THE LAST CRUSADE

THOMAS W. PETRISKO

St. Andrew's Productions

CONSECRATION AND DEDICATION

This book is consecrated to Our Lady of the Rosary and dedicated to Anatol Kaszczuk, John Haffert, and Bishop Paolo Hnilica; three of Mary's "*chosen*" ones who answered their call in heroic fashion.

Copyright © 1996 by Dr. Thomas W. Petrisko
All Rights Reserved

First Printing 1996
Second Printing 2001
ISBN: 1-891903-01-2

St. Andrew's Productions
6111 Steubenville Pike
McKees Rocks, PA 15136

Toll-Free: (888) 654-6279
Tel: (412) 787-9735
Fax: (412) 787-5204
Internet: www.saintandrew.com

Scriptural quotations are take from The Holy Bible —RSV: Catholic Edition. Alternate translations from the Latin Vulgate Bible (Douay Rheims Version —DV) are indicated when used. Some of the Scriptural quotations from the New American Bible: St. Joseph Edition, The New American Bible— Fireside Family Edition 1984-1985, The Holy Bible—Douay Rheims Edition, The New American Bible— Red Letter Edition 1986.

ACKNOWLEDGMENTS

I must first thank Our Lady and Our Lord for inspiring this effort. They did it all. This little book was truly assembled by them in so many ways!

I am indebted to the following people for their help or inspiration: Anatol Kaszczuk, John Haffert, Fr. Bill McCarthy, Sister Agnes McCormick, Fr. Robert Herrmann, Stan Karminski, Estela and Reyes Ruiz, Dr. Rosalie Turton, Bud McFarland, Robert Petrisko, Dr. Frank Novasack, Carol McElwain, Carol Brown, Amanda Ree, Jim Petrilena, Jan Connell, Linda and Audrey Santos, Ted and Maureen Flynn, Fr. Richard Foley, Fr. René Laurentin, George Malouf, The Pittsburgh Center for Peace Prayer Group and Volunteers, The Ambridge, PA. prayer group, Denis Nolan, Bishop Paolo Hnilica, Dominic & Joan Laitteri, Charlie Nole, Josyp Terelya, Eleanor Wetzel, Fr. Albert Shamon, Carlos Pontja, Luke John Hooker, Bob Schaeffer, Father Luciando Alimandi, Father Paul Sigl, Joseph Pisani (editor), John and Barb Marion, Charles Gafney, Joe and Gerry Simboli (cover design), Theresa Swango (editor), and all the attendees and speakers at the July 1996, Lay Apostolate Foundations retreat in Asbury, New Jersey.

I thank my family for the support and sacrifice they have made for this work, my wife Emily, daughters Maria, Sarah, Natasha, Dominique and my son, Joshua. As always, a special thank you to my mother and father, Andrew and Mary Petrisko and my uncle, Sam.

ABOUT THE AUTHOR

Dr. Thomas W. Petrisko was the President of the Pittsburgh Center for Peace from 1990 to 1998 and he served as editor of the Center's seven "Special Edition" newspapers. These papers, primarily featuring the apparitions and revelations of the Virgin Mary, were published in many millions throughout the world. He is the author of sixteen books, including: **The Fatima Prophecies**, *At the Doorstep of the World;* **The Face of the Father**, *An Exclusive interview with Barbara Centilli Concerning Her Revelations and Visions of God the Father;* **Glory to the Father**, *A look at the Mystical Life of Georgette Faniel;* **For the Soul of the Family**; *The Story of the Apparitions of the Virgin Mary to Estela Ruiz,* **The Sorrow, the Sacrifice and the Triumph**; *The Visions, Apparitions and Prophecies of Christina Gallagher,* **Call of the Ages**, **The Prophecy of Daniel**, **In God's Hands**; *the Miraculous Story of Little Audrey Santo,* **Mother of The Secret**, **False Prophets of Today**, **St. Joseph and the Triumph of the Saints**, **The Last Crusade**, **The Kingdom of Our Father**, **The Miracle of the Illumination, Inside Heaven and Hell** and **Inside Purgatory**.

The decree of the Congregation for the Propagation of the Faith (AAS 58, 1186 - approved by Pope Paul VI on 14 October 1966) requires that the *Nihil Obstat* and *Imprimatur* are no longer required for publications that deal with private revelations, apparitions, prophecies, miracles, etc., provided that nothing is said in contradiction of faith and morals.

The author hereby affirms his unconditional submission to whatever final judgment is delivered by the Church regarding some of the events currently under investigation in this book.

CONTENTS

FOREWORD   1
INTRODUCTION   3

1 - THE ANGELIC PSALTER   5
2 - OUR LADY OF THE ROSARY   9
3 - DECISIVE TIMES   14
4 - A MESSAGE FOR ALL HUMANITY   17
5 - "CLOSE TO THEIR FULFILLMENT"   21
6 - THE LAST APPARITIONS   25
7 - A BREAKING DAWN   31
8 - IN SEARCH OF PEACE   35
9 - TIME FOR TRUTH, TIME FOR ACTION   39
10 - "TO PREVENT THIS"   43
11 - "THE FRUIT OF ABORTION IS NUCLEAR WAR"   47
12 - "OUR LADY DOES NOT WANT NUCLEAR WAR"   53
13 - REAGAN, GORBACHEV, AND THE VIRGIN MARY   57
14 - THE QUEEN OF PEACE   62
15 - THE LAST CRUSADE   65

EPILOGUE - THE TRIUMPH OF THE LORD   70
A FINAL NOTE   72

*Lord Jesus Christ, Son of the Father,
send now Your Spirit over the earth.
Let the Holy Spirit live in the hearts of
all Nations, that they may be preserved
from degeneration, disaster and war.
May the Lady of All Nations,
who once was Mary,
be our Advocate!
Amen*

PRAYER NIHIL OBSTAT/IMPRIMATUR
Nihil Obstat: John M. T. Barton, S.T.D., L.S.S.
Censor.
Imprimatur: T. Victor Guazzelll V.G.
Westminster, 24. IX. 1970.

FOREWORD

The *Last Crusade* is a prophetic book, an apocalyptic book. It is both a warning and a clarion call. For the time is here. The kingdom is at hand. Jesus and Mary are about to usher the world into the new age—the Era of Peace after Their Triumph over the forces of darkness. The army is in place, a remnant to be sure; yet its members form a major crusade centered on the Eucharist and the Rosary that will usher in the Triumph of Mary's Immaculate Heart.

St. John Bosco's vision is about to become a full-blown reality. For the whole world is in travail, awaiting the revelations of the sons and daughters of God in this cosmic struggle between the forces of light and the forces of darkness. Satan, on the one hand, is pushing the world to the brink of nuclear disaster, while Jesus, Mary and the remnant Church—kneeling, praying and crying—are pushing back the frontiers of darkness. Yet the Catholic Church, torn by division within and assaults without, will be steadied by Mary through her Rosary and by Jesus through the Eucharist. Their Twin Hearts will Triumph.

Dr. Thomas Petrisko is a clear and prophetic voice, one of the few writers today who offers the depth of knowledge, insight and reason needed during these uncertain times. This is the *"Last Crusade"*. But the weapon, the chain that will bind the great dragon in the final battle will made up of prayer, especially the prayer of the Rosary. It is in and through the mysteries of the Rosary that we can listen to the Father's Plan, receive the love of the Son into our hearts and become empowered to live in the spirit of both Jesus and Mary. As Dr. Petrisko writes with such eloquence, the chain that binds the enemy will also be the chain that frees the children of God as they enter the Era of Peace!

Fr. Bill McCarthy, M.S.A.
My Fathers House
September 8, 1996

INTRODUCTION

The decisive times have arrived. Throughout the world, the Virgin Mary's visionaries echo her words at Fatima, *"In the end my Immaculate Heart will Triumph."*

In his best selling book, Crossing the Threshold of Hope, Pope John Paul II concurs with the visionaries that indeed, the prophecies of Fatima are *"close to their fulfillment."* But Mary's words, as well as the Pope's, repeatedly remind the faithful that a critical moment awaits the world before Fatima's Era of Peace can begin. It is a moment that may hold immense pain for God's people throughout the world. Since 1945, the world has lived in the shadow of nuclear terror and destruction. And it is this danger that could still fulfill Mary's prophetic warning at Fatima of the *"annihilation of nations."*

To *"prevent this"*, Our Lady now seeks the greatest response ever from her children. She needs prayer and reparation to bring peace. She needs a crusade for peace. She needs a Rosary Crusade that will exceed all previous efforts to date.

Along with the faithful's submission to the Lord's infinite presence in the Holy Eucharist, the voices of millions and millions in prayer will allow Heaven's Queen to secure God's victory over evil and to save the world from destruction.

Thus, let us then come together now, in fulfillment of St. John Bosco's famous prophecy, and respond to Our Lady's call one more time; one last time in order to secure a great victory. Let this crusade be *The Last Crusade*, as the Era of Divine Will dawns upon the earth and God's people rejoice in triumph with their Savior.

"I say to all the people who find it difficult to accept my messages and those of my Son, pray the Rosary from your heart, all three mysteries, for nine days. Offer up these prayers to my Son's Heart and to the Holy Spirit for enlightenment. If you do that you will understand."

The Blessed Virgin Mary
to Christina Gallagher,
February 4, 1988, County Mayo, Ireland
From *The Sorrow, the Sacrifice, and the Triumph*

Chapter One

THE ANGELIC PSALTER

On the wall of the Sistine Chapel, Michelangelo's *Last Judgement* is an awe-inspiring yet intimidating painting of the power and glory of God. Completed in the year 1541, its newly refurbished finish projects the story of salvation like no other.

Coming at a time of crisis in the Church, the painting was a message from Michelangelo to the Bishops and Cardinals who met at the Council of Trent in 1545. Their task was to initiate the counter - Reformation which would resolidify the Church's doctrines and teachings. And all around them, they found in Michelangelo's work the inspiration to do so.

Most significantly, the *Last Judgement* incorporated in its visual message those doctrines that forever imprinted the Church's position on Mary, the Mother of God and the honor given to her as such.

Indeed, Michelangelo's great fresco held out for all to see with their own eyes that Mary is forever at the side of her Son, reigning as Heaven's Queen and earth's model of discipleship. And Michelangelo's painting was not to be lacking in the depth of this message, for he painted a huge Rosary hanging down over the ramparts of Heaven on which two souls can be seen grasping and pulling their way up into Paradise.

No message through word or image tells us better how important the Rosary is in the lives of the faithful. For heaven has been calling souls to understand and implement this mystery of salvation for centuries.

The prayer of the Rosary is said to have begun in the year

1214 when the Virgin Mary appeared to St. Dominic and presented to him the Rosary as a powerful means of converting the Albigensians and other sinners.

The Albigensian heresy rocked the thirteenth century Church in a frightful way. In a forest outside the city of Toulouse, Mary reportedly came to St. Dominic after he prayed for three days and nights and eventually, because of self inflicted penances, lapsed into a coma.

At this point, the Virgin appeared to him and said,

> *"Dear Dominic, do you know which weapon the Blessed Trinity wants to use to reform the world?"*
> *"Oh, my Lady,"* replied St. Dominic, *You know far better than I do because next to your Son Jesus Christ you have always been the chief instrument of our salvation."* Upon this, Mary gave St. Dominic the Rosary, explaining to him that it was *"the foundation stone of the New Testament."*

At once, the great saint returned to Toulouse, where he preached with zeal the merits of the new prayer. Solidified and assisted by angels, his sermon was accompanied by the roar of heavenly thunder, as reportedly the sky drew dark and the earth shook while flashes of lightening laced the heavens.
As fear embraced the crowd, an image of Mary reportedly revealed itself to be raising its arms up and down to heaven as if to call down God's vengeance upon the people if they failed to convert. After this, most of the town is said to have converted and the prayer of the Rosary then began to spread.

St. Dominic preached the Rosary the rest of his life, but two centuries later the prayer almost disappeared. However, in the year 1460, after receiving a warning from the Lord Himself, Blessed Alan de la Roche reportedly led a resurgence of the prayer.

Blessed Alan was given in vision to understand how Jesus and Mary repeatedly came to St. Dominic to help him refine his understanding of the power of the Rosary. And how heaven wished this prayer become firmly embraced by the faithful as their preferred weapon in combating evil.

Blessed Alan also received visions of Jesus and Mary and even St. Dominic, as he resurrected and reestablished the Rosary throughout Europe.

Thus, along with the Sacraments, the faithful were being guided in the way heaven wished souls to spiritually survive in a world coming under a great siege by Satan and his followers. Indeed, Mary began to reveal that a spiritual war was unfolding, and the Rosary was to be the ultimate weapon for this conflict.

After Blessed Alan de la Roche restored the prayer in 1460, the Rosary became known as the Psalter of Jesus and Mary. This is because it has the same number of Angelic Salutations as there are Psalms in the Book of Psalms.

In his book, *The Secret of the Rosary*, St. Louis de Montfort explains why the Rosary is so powerful,

> *"Since simple and uneducated people are not able to say the Psalms of David, the Rosary is held to be just as fruitful for them as David's Psalter is for others. But the Rosary can be considered to be even more valuable than the latter for three reasons:*
>
> *1. Firstly, because the Angelic Psalter bears a nobler fruit, that of the Word Incarnate, whereas David's Psalter only prophecies His (Christ's) coming;*
> *2. Secondly, just as the real thing is more important than its prefiguration and as the body is more than its shadow, in the same way the Psalter of Our Lady is greater than David's Psalter which did no more than prefigured it;*

> 3. *And thirdly, because Our Lady's Psalter (or the Rosary made up of the Our Father and Hail Mary) is the direct work of the Most Blessed Trinity and was not made through a human instrument.*

The Virgin Mary's Psalter or Rosary is divided into three parts of five decades each for the following reasons:

1. To honor the three Persons of the Most Blessed Trinity;
2. To honor the life, death and glory of Jesus Christ;
3. To imitate the Church Triumphant, to help the members of the Church Militant and to lessen the pains of the Church Suffering;
4. To imitate the three groups into which the Psalms are divided:
   a) The first being for the purgative life,
   b) the second for the illuminative life,
   c) and the third for the unitive life;
5. And, finally, to give us graces in abundance during our lifetime, peace at death, and glory in eternity.

The word Rosary means *"Crown of Roses,"* and thus, whenever a person devoutly prays the Rosary, they place a crown of one hundred and fifty-three red roses and sixteen white roses on the heads of Jesus and Mary. Blessed Alan taught these mysteries of the Rosary and its promises. And he began to assemble an association, like an army, whose members would pledge to pray the Rosary and spread its devotion.

Most incredibly, by the time Blessed Alan de la Roche died on September 8, 1475, (the Church celebrated birthday of Mary), over one hundred thousand people had entered into the *Confraternity of the Rosary.*

Chapter Two

OUR LADY OF THE ROSARY

Over the centuries, many great kings, popes, and saints courageously spread the Rosary, often recording its miraculous power of securing heavens favors for both small and great successes.

St. Phillip Neri, St. Bernard, St. Robert Bellarmine, St. Francis de Sales, St. Bonaventure, St. Gertrude, St. Ignatius Loyola, St. Teresa of Avilla, and St. Louis de Montfort all became champions of the Rosary.

But it was especially St. Louis de Montfort who explained and forwarded the Rosary's powers and mysteries. These are the mysteries of Christ's life, death and resurrection on earth. Mysteries that especially included His Mother. Most of all, St. Louis de Montfort, established how necessary it was to contemplate the mysteries of the Rosary in order to fully use the prayer to its fullest potential.

Wrote St. de Montfort in his book, *The Secret of the Rosary*:

> *"For, in reality, the Rosary said without meditating on the sacred mysteries of our salvation would be almost like a body without a soul: excellent matter but without the form which is meditation—this latter being that which sets it apart from all other devotions.*
>
> *"The first part of the Rosary contains five mysteries: the first is the Annunciation of the Archangel Saint Gabriel to Our Lady; the second, the Visitation of Our Lady to her cousin Saint Elizabeth; the third, the Nativity of Jesus Christ; the fourth, the Presentation of the Child Jesus in the*

temple and the Purification of Our Lady; and the fifth, the Finding of Jesus in the Temple among the doctors.

"These are called the JOYFUL MYSTERIES because of the joy which they gave to the whole universe. Our Lady and the angels were overwhelmed with joy the moment when the Son of God was incarnate. Saint Elizabeth and Saint John the Baptist were filled with joy by the visit of Jesus and Mary. Heaven and earth rejoiced at the birth of Our Savior. Holy Simeon felt great consolation and was filled with joy when he took the Holy Child in his arms. The doctors were lost in admiration and wonderment at the answers which Jesus gave and how could anyone describe the joy of Mary and Joseph when they found the Child Jesus after He has been lost for three days?

"The second part of the Rosary is also composed of five mysteries which are called the SORROWFUL MYSTERIES because they show us Our Lord weighed down with sadness, covered with wounds, laden with insults, sufferings and torments. The first of these mysteries is Jesus' Prayer and Agony in the Garden of Olives; the second, His Scourging; the third, His Crowning with Thorns; the fourth, Jesus carrying His Cross; and the fifth, His Crucifixion and Death on Mount Calvary.

"The third part of the Rosary contains five other mysteries which are called the GLORIOUS MYSTERIES because when we say them we meditate on Jesus and Mary in their triumph and glory. The first is the Resurrection of Jesus Christ; the second, His Ascension into heaven; the third, the Descent of the Holy Ghost upon the Apostles; the fourth, Our Lady's glorious Assumption into heaven; and the fifth, her Crowning in Heaven."

Thus, praying of the Holy Rosary, together with meditating

on its sacred mysteries, is a sacrifice of praise to God in thanks for the great graces of our redemption. It is also, says St. Louis de Montfort, a holy reminder of the sufferings, death and glory of Jesus Christ, all of which are perfect for the spiritual maturity of a soul. Therefore, a soul who faithfully recites the Rosary is given the following graces:

1) A perfect knowledge of Jesus Christ.
2) A purification of soul, washing away sin.
3) Victory over enemies.
4) An increased ease in the practice of virtue.
5) A love for Jesus Christ.
6) An enrichment in graces and merits.
7) The graces necessary to pay all our debts to God and our fellow men.

Over the centuries, Mary revealed how the Rosary melts the most hardened hearts, the greatest sinners. The Rosary invites, she says, a fervor for God and produces change in lives. Most of all, Mary says it appeases God's wrath.

Indeed, it is this need the Virgin often invokes when imploring the Rosary. For both individual souls and nations, Mary pleads for the faithful to pray her Rosary to restrain the arm of her Son's coming justice.

While some dispute the origination of the Rosary with St. Dominic, five Popes have credited him with its founding. And although its full history is somewhat a mystery, the accounts of its numerous successes are not.

Just thirty years after the Council of Trent's initial meeting, off the coast of Greece at the Gulf of Lepanto, a greatly outnumbered force of Christian defenders held off a Turkish invasion on October 7, 1571. It was considered a miraculous victory brought about specifically through the Rosary, for St. Pius V's Rosary Crusade united all of Europe in prayer. From this, the

Feast of the Most Holy Rosary was established in 1573 and is still celebrated to this day on October 7th.

Even before the battle of Lepanto, the Rosary was credited with bringing a miraculous victory in 1474 to the city of Cologne, which was under attack by Bergundian Troops. After Lepanto, another victory over the Turks at Peterwardein in Hungary, by Prince Eugene on August 5, 1716, the Feast of Our Lady of the Snows, led Pope Clement XI to extend the Feast of the most Holy Rosary to the Universal Church.

By the nineteenth century, so numerous were the miraculous favors credited to the Rosary, that Popes began to recognize the Rosary as an institution within the Catholic Church. During his 25 year reign (1878-1903), Pope Leo XIII wrote Twelve encyclicals on the Rosary and its devotion. Pope Leo especially attempted to use the Rosary to bring unity to the Church. His writings also "officially" credited the Rosary with the Church's victories of the past.

In *Supremi Apostolatus*, Pope Leo XIII began the recognition of the month of October as the month of special devotion to the Rosary. In his encyclical *Salutaris ille*, published on December 24, 1883, Pope Leo called upon each family to recite the Rosary "*daily*". And in his letter of September 20, 1887 he elevated the nature of the feast day to what it is today.

Most significantly, in his September 1892 encyclical, *Magnae Del Matris*, Pope Leo XIII stressed the importance of the Rosary as the most appropriate form of prayer to Mary, and that through the Rosary the great mysteries of the faith can be unlocked. In his 25 years, Pope Leo XIII touched on all aspects of the Rosary devotion, elevating it in a landmark way in the history of the Church, and setting the stage for the 20th century devotion to Mary that would especially come from her apparitions.

In her last apparition at Fatima, on October 13, 1917, the Virgin Mary told the children that she was **"Our Lady of the**

Rosary". Appearing with the Rosary in her right hand and the Scapular in her left, the Virgin invoked the memory of what history relays she once told St. Dominic centuries before — ***"one day the Rosary and the Scapular will save the world."***

And that day is today! Beginning with her apparitions at Rue Du Bac, Paris in 1830 all the way till the present, the modern era of Mary and her "Rosary Crusade" is evident.

From Lourdes in 1858, where she called for penance and the Rosary, to Pontmain on January 17, 1871, where the children reported that each time the people prayed the Rosary, the image of Mary in the sky increased in size, Mary has continuously invoked the Rosary in almost all of her apparitions.

Foretelling at Fatima a dangerous future for the entire world, the Queen of the Most Holy Rosary made it clear; the Rosary would be the solution to a world headed into the atomic age. For there was coming a critical time in the history of the world, a time when "annihilation" could be just moments away. And the faithful needed to be prepared for the decisive moments.

Are we now in those decisive times?

Through the eyes of faith, let us closely examine this question. For God has placed a great responsibility on the faithful of this generation. It is a responsibility that will determine and shape the future of mankind. And like the villagers of Toulouse, heaven is waiting for an answer.

Chapter Three

DECISIVE TIMES

On June 24, 1981, the Blessed Virgin Mary began appearing to six children in the mountain village of Medjugorje in the former nation of Yugoslavia. Preceded by a flash of light, Mary introduced herself as the "**Queen of Peace**", and told the children not to fear. She came, she said, with a message of peace for the world,

> *"Peace, Peace, Peace! Be reconciled! Make peace with God and with each other!...Without you, dear children, I cannot help the world...help me!...Pray, Pray, Pray!...Give time to the Rosary...I have come to call the world to conversion for the last time...tell the whole world, tell it without delay, be converted and do not wait!"*

That was over fifteen years ago. Today many believe the decisive times have arrived. The times that Mary's urgent words at Fatima and Medjugorje were intended to forewarn.

But what are the reasons to believe we are in such times and that God will soon act to bring a change in the world, the change Mary prophesied at Fatima when she foretold **"an era of peace."**

To answer this, let us go back in time. Since 1830, there have been literally dozens of apparitions of the Virgin Mary. And while only a handful are recognized as worthy of faith by the Church, Mary has repeatedly foretold through her visitations the coming of a critical time in the history of the world.

But at Fatima in 1917, Mary not only left a serious warning, but also announced there would come a climax to her admonitions. And, she promised, this climax would result in a new era of peace for the world.

This is significant. For at Fatima, the following prophecies were given and have been fulfilled:

1) World War I would soon end—*The war ended in 1918.*
2) Francisco and Jacinta, two of the visionaries at Fatima, would soon go to heaven. *Both children died within several years of the apparitions.*
3) A great evil would come out of Russia. *This evil was seen to be Communism.*
4) The great evil (Communism) would spread throughout the world. *This has occurred over the last 80 years.*
5) This evil would foment wars. *As a result of Communism, many wars spread throughout the world and continue to this day.*
6) A great miracle would occur on October 13, 1917. *The Miracle of the Sun occurred before an estimated 70,000 witnesses at Fatima on the predicted day.*
7) There would be a second great war. *World War II began in the late 1930's and ended in 1945.*
8) A great sign would be given to the world before the Second World War. *This great sign, an unnatural illumination of the sky, was given on January 25-26, 1938, according to Sister Lucia, the surviving visionary of Fatima.*
9) The Holy Father would have much to suffer. *John Paul II was shot on the anniversary of Fatima, May 13, 1981.*
10) Persecution of the Church. *Intensive persecution of the Church has occurred worldwide. Behind the Iron Curtain and in the Far East, tens of thousands of churches closed and millions were persecuted, killed or jailed for their faith.*

From the prophecies given by Mary at Fatima, only two remain unfulfilled:

1) Various nations will be "**annihilated**."
2) There will come in the end,"**the Triumph of the Immaculate Heart and the Era of Peace**"—which will follow the complete fall of atheism (communism) in Russia.

Thus, the answer to the original question, *Are we now in the decisive times?"* can be reduced to whether or not the two remaining Fatima prophecies are near fulfillment.

For if they are, this would signify that Mary's *"warnings"* at Fatima and her *"pleas"* at Medjugorje are now at the doorstep of the world.

Chapter Four

A MESSAGE FOR ALL HUMANITY

The facts to support the belief that the remaining prophecies of Fatima will soon be fulfilled are difficult to establish unequivocally. However, circumstantial evidence is strong.

The first key is the Pope. Pope John Paul II is said to be convinced that now is the time for the fulfillment of Fatima. In his 1995 book, *Crossing the Threshold of Hope,* the Holy Father writes,

> "....Mary appeared to the three children at Fatima in Portugal and spoke to them words that now, at the end of this century, seem close to their fulfillment."

Experts say, this conviction of Pope John Paul II's became firm as he recovered from the attempted assassination on May 13, 1981. Father Malachi Martin, in his book, *The Keys of This Blood* (Touchstone, 1990), outlines in detail the facts concerning the development of the Holy Father's convictions:

> "As he convalesced in the Policlinico Gemelli that August, the concrete facts of the situation worked a change of attitude in John Paul. Those facts were the growing crisis in Poland between Solidarity and the government, the new twist in Moscow's attitude to Solidarity, as something dangerous and to be crushed; the gap left by Wyszynski's death, a gap that the new Primate of Poland, Jozef Cardinal

Glemp, could not fill; the significance of his own attempted assassination on May 13, feast day of Our Lady of Fatima, and—as he firmly believed—his own deliverance from sudden death by Agca's bullets through the protection of Mary as Our Lady of Fatima.

"*John Paul could not put all those details into a coherent order without coming to the conclusion that the geopolitical timetable was much shorter than he and Cardinal Wyszynski had thought. The (for him) obvious intervention of Mary in preserving his life placed him—in his own eyes—in a direct relationship with Fatima and its 'Third Secret.' If there was one dominant element in that 'Third Secret', it was Russia. The provisos of the 'Third Secret' made sense only in relation to Russia.*

"*He had accepted as fact that John XXIII's decision not to do as the 'Third Secret' asked—to publish the actual text, and to undertake a collegial consecration of Russia to Mary—had placed the Church and therefore the world in the 'or' situation. He had accepted the predictions of dire physical and spiritual chastisement. He had assumed—up to that August of 1981—they were gridded on a long, drawn-out timetable. Now he realized that the geopolitical change implied by the 'Third Secret' was not far off. It was imminent. It was about to take place. Russia was its womb. Russia was its focal point. Russia was to be the main agent of change. Russia was to be the source of a universal blindness and error.*"

After personally studying the Third Secret of Fatima and dispatching aides to interview Fatima experts and Sister Lucia herself, we know for certain Pope John Paul II took action—strong and deliberate action.

Malachi Martin says the Holy Father became convinced the

events unfolding in Poland were related to the state of world affairs and possibly to the contents of the undisclosed Third Secret of Fatima.

Consequently, in 1982 and 1984, the Holy Father initiated and led consecrations of the world to the Immaculate Heart of Mary. Consecrations intended to fulfill the Virgin's requests at Fatima.

In addition, between those two dates of the consecrations, a message was conveyed to Pope John Paul II by Father Tomislav Vlasic of Medjugorje on December 16, 1983. This message outlined the Virgin's warnings at Medjugorje and some of what is known relating to the contents of the Ten Secrets as given at Medjugorje to the visionary Mirjana Dragicevic-Soldo. However, it is not known if this report had any significance on the Pope's thinking. But Pope John Paul II has been repeatedly reported by numerous priests and bishops to be a believer in the apparitions at Medjugorje. And a message to Maria Pavlovic, another Medjugorje visionary, on November 30, 1983, reflects the Virgin's interest in the Holy Father's awareness of how crucial time now was in the world:

> ***"You must warn the Bishop very soon, and the Pope, with respect to the urgent and the great importance of the message for all humanity...The peace of the world is in a state of crisis. Become brothers among you, increase prayer and fasting in order to be saved."*** *(The Blessed Virgin Mary to Marija Pavlovic, Medjugorje, Yugoslavia, November 30, 1983).*

Once again, this is only circumstantial evidence. But it certainly appears to indicate the contents of the Third Secret of Fatima loomed heavily on the Holy Father's mind. And Medjugorje's message of urgency may have done nothing to lessen this situation.

In addition, on April 22, 1984, after consultation with the Holy See, Bishop John Shojiro Ito of Nigata, Japan, fully approved the apparitions of Akita, Japan. These 1973 apparitions carried with them, once again, an urgent message. It was a message which, like at Fatima, foretold *"annihilation"* if the world did not convert. Together, with the message of Fatima, and possibly Medjugorje, the urgency of the situation upon the Pope is said to have grown.

Since 1984, the Pope's words and actions do nothing to change this view. In the January-February 1994 issue of *Voice of the Sacred Hearts,* Pope John Paul II is quoted as saying Mary's apparitions now are "*A sign of the times...of terrible times.*"

Chapter Five

"CLOSE TO THEIR FULFILLMENT"

As Marian experts note, the Pope's words in *Crossing the Threshold of Hope* literally echo the Virgin Mary's words to almost all her most prominent visionaries in the world today.

Thus, from what we know about the Third Secret of Fatima and from the known message of Akita, along with the Pope's words and actions, it appears the time for the fulfillment of Fatima's remaining prophecies is rapidly approaching. The Pope further signaled this conviction by his efforts to give Mary credit for the *fall* of communism. On December 30, 1990, *Time* Magazine wrote,

> *"Moreover, John Paul is firmly convinced, as are many others, that Mary brought an end to communism throughout Europe. His faith is rooted in the famed prophecies of Mary at Fatima in 1917. According to Sister Lucia, one of the children who claimed to see her, the Virgin predicted the rise of Soviet totalitarianism before it happened. In a subsequent vision, she directed the Pope and his bishops to consecrate Russia to her Immaculate Heart in order to bring communism to an end."*

With the fall of communism, much of the remaining circumstantial evidence and related facts appear to uphold the belief that the remaining Fatima prophecies are close to fulfillment. As are perhaps some long awaited Scriptural prophecies. Let us look at this evidence by pondering several questions.

1) *Would the Holy Father indicate his concern so much if he felt the remaining prophesied events were not imminent?* In his book, *The Keys to This Blood*, Malachi Martin says the Holy Father was unsure of Fatima's time table prior to his attempted assassination. Afterwards, the Pope's words seemed to echo Our Lady's words at many of her contemporary apparitions, messages which Mary declares are **"urgent."** The Holy Father said on May 13, 1982, one year after his attempted assassination: *"Mary's message is still more relevant than it was 65 years ago. It is still more urgent."*

2) *Would all the apparitions, miracles, signs, healings, and messages given to the world in the last two decades be said by visionaries to be so urgent if God was not going to now fulfill His plan?* Many renown Marian writers say it is hard to believe all of Mary's activity around the world in the last fifteen years will be left unfulfilled, delayed or cancelled. Likewise, it is also hard to believe the Virgin would speak of **"urgency"** if the present times were truly not urgent. Mary indicated recently that many people who converted to God are falling back to their old ways and are becoming confused or doubtful. This is something she foretold early on at Medjugorje: **"I know many will not believe you, and that many who have an impassioned faith will cool off."** (Medjugorje, 1983) Therefore, if everything Mary said was to be cancelled or delayed, this would perhaps make, in effect, much of her effort to this point moot. In addition, the next generation would have to somehow respond and fulfill her messages. Certainly by then, the world will be quite distant to the present supernatural events and the feeling of urgency the Virgin brought at Medjugorje when she said **"do not delay."**

3) *Are all the natural disasters, wars, and freakish weather just a strange cycle, or is God trying to tell us something?* Even atmospheric science experts say all of this is unparalleled. Weather records of all kinds are being broken everywhere and social scientists say there has never been as many wars raging as now and in the last 80 years. Domestic violence and family turmoil are at unprecedented levels. These events certainly add great credit to the many contemporary prophecies of Mary's that state we are at the **"end of an era"** and these are the **"signs."** Indeed, Mary's own words, to almost all of her present day visionaries say we must recognize the **"Signs of the Times."** The signs, as the Pope said, of "*our times.*"

4) *Since God wishes us to have faith in His words, which He has marked with numerous signs and miracles varying from physical healings to thousands of rosaries turning gold, is it likely God would not fulfill so many prophecies that insist He will now act? In addition, the messages assure the faithful and the innocent that God's justice is inescapable. With the vast amount of genocide, abortion, violence, and nonconformity to His laws as is now occurring, is it likely God will allow all of this to continue?* One has to suspect not. Likewise, the Virgin Mary says God's justice must now come. This is especially evident in the Church approved message of Akita, Japan. Without claiming to know God's mind, it is almost inconceivable much more injustice will be allowed. Because of science, mankind has the ability to not only destroy the young and the old, but the entire world rather methodically. But most of all, there appears to be too much injustice to the innocent now occurring and God always defends the innocent. Scripture tells us **"He hears their cry."** This is especially true for the unborn. As the Holy

Father stated on September 1, 1996, *"A nation that kills its own children is without hope."* Even without private revelation, people of all faiths seem to sense the world has gone astray and God will soon right it. Mary's messages seem to insist this will happen soon. Indeed, the vast majority of her messages do not even speak of an extended delay. They speak of mitigation of the chastisement through prayer and reparation but not delay in God's plan to convert the world, end the misery, and bring His Triumph. At Fatima, Mary asserted, **"In the end Russia will be converted and an era of peace will be granted to the world."** Like the Pope, few who seriously study Fatima's message believe **"in the end"** will occur after the year 2000 A.D.

But once again, it is only through the light of faith that one can truly grasp the significance of our times. And it is in Mary's words where we best find this light. For the Queen of Heaven announced these will be her last apparitions, and therefore, her last words to her earthly children.

Chapter Six

THE LAST APPARITIONS

To accompany Pope John Paul II's declaration, all of the circumstantial evidence, and the *"signs of the times"* are Mary's words of urgency over the last fifteen years. Could there be any suggestion in the Virgin's revelations that God may change His plan and bring the Era of Peace at some later date? Or Is the Virgin clearly indicating in her words God will soon act?

Let us examine some of Mary's messages to help us look for the answers to these questions. These messages are on different subjects, yet presented here to show it appears Heaven intends to soon bring a change in the world, the change Mary foretold at Fatima.

Concerning Mary's apparitions at Medjugorje:
1) Mirjana Soldo: *(one of the visionaries at Medjugorje)*: "She (Mary) said that she stayed with us for a long time, longer than is necessary, but that this is the last apparition on earth
Father Vlasic: *What do you mean, 'the last apparition on earth?'*
Mirjana: *It is the last time Jesus or Mary will appear on earth.*
Father Vlasic: *What do you mean 'appear?'*
Mirjana: *The last time they will appear as they have so that you can speak with them.*
Father Vlasic: *You mean that this is the last apparition in this era, in this period of the Church, or that they will never again come to earth?*

Mirjana: *I don't know. The Madonna said this is the last apparition on earth."* (Source: *Heart of the Message of Medjugorje*, Mark Miravalle, S.T.D., 1988)

2) Janice T. Connell: *Do you know if this is the Blessed Mother's last apparition on earth?*
Marija Pavlovic: "*Yes. The Blessed Mother said that this is her last apparition on earth, where we can touch her, see her, and talk to her.*" (Source, *Queen of the Cosmos*, Janice T. Connell 1991)

3) In November of 1982, someone asked Mirjana why Our Lady has come here so often and for such a long time. Without hesitation Mirjana answered: *"'Because these are her last apparitions.' Mirjana also said that Our Lady told them that when these apparitions come to an end, there will be false apparitions in the world and we must be very careful not to be deceived."*

Opinions have been expressed from many sides, even from the Franciscans in Medjugorje, whether or not it can be true the apparitions in Medjugorje will be the last apparitions of Our Lady in the world.

But on May 2, 1982, Medjugorje visionary Vicka Ivankovic was asked what she knew about this and she answered: 'During the apparition, *Our Lady literally said this:* **I have come to convert people for the last time. I will not come to earth anymore.**'

And in order to remove any doubts, on June 25, 1982, the first anniversary of the apparitions, Father Tomislav Vlasic asked Medjugorje visionary Ivan Dragicevic to ask Our Lady two questions: *Is this apparition of Our Lady in Medjugorje the last one? Our Lady didn't answer.*

And then the second question: *Are these apparitions the last ones in the present world? Our Lady answered:* **"These are the last apparitions."** One anonymous priest associated closely with the apparitions said, *"I think that Our Lady removed all doubt with her answer. Not only the apparitions in Medjugorje by themselves, but all other apparitions of the Mother of God which appear at this time in the world, are the last apparitions in this world."* (Source: Queen of Peace in Medjugorje, Jacov Martin, 1989)

Concerning Conversion:

Message from the Virgin Mary to Medjugorje visionary Mirjana Soldo (given on Mirjana's birthday).

"One more time, I beseech all of you to pray, to help by your prayers the unbelievers, those who do not have the grace to experience God in their hearts with a living faith. I do not want to threaten again! My wish is just to warn you all as a Mother. I beg you for people who do not know about the secrets...I want to tell you how I suffer for all because I am the Mother of All." (March 18, 1989 at Medjugorje)

Concerning Fatima:

Monthly message from the Virgin Mary to Medjugorje visionary Maria Pavlovic.

"Dear Children! Today also, I invite you to pray, now as never before, when my plan has begun to be realized. Satan is strong and wants to sweep away plans of peace and joy and make you think that my Son is not strong in His decisions. Therefore, I call all of you, dear children, to pray and fast still more firmly. I invite you to renunciation for nine days so that with your help, everything I wanted to realize through the secrets I began in Fatima may be fulfilled. I call you, dear children, to grasp the importance of my coming and the seriousness of the situation. I want to save all souls and present them to God. Therefore, let us pray

that everything I have begun be fully realized. Thank you for having responded to my call." (August 25, 1991, Source: *Our Lady Queen of Peace* newspaper, Special Edition II, Pittsburgh Center For Peace)

Concerning Medjugorje:
Message from the Virgin Mary to Maria Pavlovic, Medjugorje.
"Medjugorje is a sign to all of you and a call to pray and live the days of grace that God is giving you." (April 25, 1992, Source: *Medjugorje Gebetsaktion*, 1992)

Concerning the Apostasy and Priests:
Message from the Virgin Mary to Father Stefano Gobbi, Italy.
"Behold: when everything will have come tumbling down, all that will remain will be the strength of their tears that will compel me to intervene in an amazing and terrible way. And my Triumph will begin with these beloved sons, my priests." (February 23, 1974 - Source: *To The Priests, Our Lady's Beloved Sons*)

Concerning the World:
Message from the Virgin Mary to Father Stefano Gobbi, Italy.
1) *"A new world must be born, completely renewed, by the Light and Love of my Son, Jesus."* (November 1, 1973, Source: *To The Priests, Our Lady's Beloved Sons*)

Message from the Virgin Mary to Father Stefano Gobbi, Italy.
2) *"Now you are living in that period of time when the Red Dragon, that is to say Marxist atheism, is spreading throughout the whole world and is increasingly bringing about the ruin of souls.*

"He is indeed succeeding in seducing and casting down a third of the stars of heaven.

"These stars, in the firmament of the Church, are the pastors: they are yourselves, my poor priest-sons.

"Has not perchance even the Vicar of my Son affirmed to you that it is the dearest friends, even the conferees of the same table, the priests and the religious, who are today betraying and setting themselves against the Church?" (May 13, 1976 - Source: *To The Priests, Our Lady's Beloved Sons*)

Message from the Virgin Mary to Father Stefano Gobbi, Italy.

3) *"Decisive moments draw near, great events await you."* (December 31, 1973 - Source: *To The Priests, Our Lady's Beloved Sons*)

Message from Our Lady to Father Stefano Gobbi, Italy.

4) *"Marxist atheism will contaminate everything; like a poisonous fog it will penetrate everywhere and will bring many of my children to death of faith.*

"It will subvert the truth contained in the Gospel. It will deny the divine nature of my Son and the divine origin of the Church. Above all, it will threaten its hierarchial structure and attempt to break down the Rock upon which the edifice of the Church is built." (November 9, 1975 - Source: *To The Priests, Our Lady's Beloved Sons*)

Concerning Mary:

Message from the Virgin Mary to Father Stefano Gobbi, Italy.

"At the moment of its greatest confusion, on the very eve of events which will upset the faith of so many of my children, this is the sign which I will give: My very self!" (December 7, 1974 - Source: *To The Priests, Our Lady's Beloved Sons*)

Concerning Time:

Message from the Virgin Mary to Father Stefano Gobbi, Italy.

1) ***"The time left at your disposal is now short."*** (January 28, 1975 - Source: *To The Priests, Our Lady's Beloved Sons*)

Message from Our Lady to Father Stefano Gobbi, Italy.

2) ***"I am pressed for time."*** (April 29, 1977 - Source: *To The Priests, Our Lady's Beloved Sons*)

Message from the Virgin Mary to Father Stefano Gobbi, Italy.

3) ***"Some of you will have no more time, because the number which the Heavenly Father has determined will have been completed."*** (October 1, 1977 - Source: *To The Priests, Our Lady's Beloved Sons*)

Message from the Virgin Mary to Father Stefano Gobbi, Italy.

4) **"My message is now more urgent and timely than ever. Timely, because never as in these moments has humanity found itself so close to the brink of its own destruction; and urgent, because that which the justice of God has decreed is now in the process of being quickly realized.**

   "Beloved children, let all of you heed the anguished appeal of your Mother: turn back along the road which leads to God through prayer and conversion." (December 31, 1977 - Source: *To The Priests, Our Lady's Beloved Sons*)

Chapter Seven

A BREAKING DAWN

The Virgin Mary has especially given to the world messages concerning the present and the future. Here are some of the most detailed revelations which further confirm we are in the decisive times.

Concerning the Present:
Message from the Virgin Mary to Father Stefano Gobbi, Italy.
"I assure you that what I already foretold you at Fatima has truly come to pass: Russia has spread its errors throughout the whole world. The Lord has made use of godless nations to chastise the Christian peoples who have left the path marked out by my Son Jesus.

"Offer up the holocaust of your suffering. The hours through which you are living are truly difficult and painful. That which is awaiting you is suffering such as the world has never known.

"Yet, through this holocaust, you are able to save those who are seeking your ruin, and you are able to do good to those who are, for you, a scourge.

"Thus, even these great nations which have openly rebelled against God and have become a veritable scourge for all humanity can, in the end, be saved."
(June 16, 1978 - Source: *To The Priests, Our Lady's Beloved Sons*)

Concerning the Future:
Message from the Virgin Mary to Father Stefano Gobbi, Italy

"You have entered into the conclusive period of the Great Tribulation, and the hour of the great trial, of which I have been foretelling you for so many years, has now arrived for you. It is a trial so great and painful, that you cannot even imagine it, but it is necessary for the Church and for all humanity, in order that the new era, the new world, and the reconciliation of humanity with their Lord, may come upon you." (February 2, 1991 - Source: *To The Priests, Our Lady's Beloved Sons*)

Concerning the Future:
 Message from the Virgin Mary to Christina Gallagher, Ireland.
 "Tell all humanity to prepare themselves, the time has come for the cleansing of all humanity." (January 30, 1991 - Source: *Call of the Ages*)

Concerning the Future:
 Message from the Virgin Mary to Sister Natalie, Hungary.
 "Await with a penitent soul the coming of the great age which is getting closer and closer with each day." (January 31, 1987 - Source: *The Victorious Queen of the World*)

Concerning the Future:
 Message from the Virgin Mary to Josyp Terelya, Ukraine.
 "The times are coming which are spoken of as the end times, as has been foretold." (May 11, 1987 - Source: *Witness*)

Concerning the Present:
 Message from the Virgin Mary to Estela Ruiz, U.S.A.
 "...More than ever, as you begin to see the SIGNS

OF THE TIMES, you need to know God's love for you. Yes, my children, God loves you even when many in the world do not acknowledge or recognize Him. He loves man even when many turn against Him." (February 5, 1994 released message.)

Concerning the Future:
Message from the Virgin Mary to Patricia Talbot, Ecuador.
"Little children, know that all that you do benefits the world. Your prayers, penances and fasts are helping to prevent the Third World War. Everything is as I have told you. All is in your hands. From you it depends whether the Chastisement will be as strong as the pain that my Son feels or that the Chastisement will be diminished by prayer." (1990 - Source: *I am the Guardian of the Faith*)

Concerning the Future:
Message from the Virgin Mary to Sister Agnes Sassagawa - Akita, Japan.
"Those who place their confidence in me will be saved." (Source: *Akita, the Tears and Messages of Mary*)

Concerning the Future:
Message from Jesus to Madeleine - Dozule, France.
"I tell you truly the time has come for the world to repent, for a universal change is near, such as has never been from the beginning of the world until this day; and will never be again." (1983 Source: *Dozule: the Unique and Definitive Message of Christ.*)

In addition to Our Lady's messages from her many apparitions, the Virgin has marked her words with numerous miracles from God to sustain and authenticate their truth. Thus, from these messages, and certainly the other related facts, the evidence is strong that God will soon act. Indeed, through the eyes of faith, it appears the decisive times have arrived.

However, like the children of Fatima, Jesus and Mary assure today's visionaries that those who respond to God's call to conversion have nothing to fear. By praying and living the messages, peace will reign in their hearts. Indeed, Mary reminds us we are in God's hands and will share in the Triumph. As she told Father Stefano Gobbi on December 8, 1993,

> *"These are the years when Satan is ruling as a sure victor; these are therefore also the years of my Triumph. My light will become stronger and stronger the more you enter into the decisive moments of the battle. In the end, the victory will be that of your Immaculate Mother who, with her virginal foot, will crush the head of the serpent and with her hands will bind the great dragon, that he may thus be rendered powerless and no longer be able to do harm in the world.*
>
> *"Both humanity and the Church will experience this new era, which you are now awaiting in confidence and in prayer, in suffering and in hope.*
>
> *"For this, as a breaking dawn, you will as of today see my light becoming stronger and stronger, until it encircles the whole earth, ready now to open itself to the new day, which will begin with the Triumph of my Immaculate Heart in the world."*

Chapter Eight

IN SEARCH OF PEACE

From the Virgin Mary's apparitions, we understand her call to peace, prayer and conversion is crucial in order for mankind to obtain peace. This peace, Mary says, is a peace that must start with the individual and then, through faith and prayer, spread throughout the world to all nations and peoples.

At Medjugorje, we particularly see the Madonna's message as a pure reflection of Scripture. Over the years, her messages there have reminded us of Our Lord's Gospel teachings and how Church tradition is designed to enhance these teachings in our life so as to produce the happiness and peace all men seek.

As the well-known Franciscan priest at Medjugorje, Father Jozo Zovko, stated in the book *A Man Called Jozo*, (The Riehle Foundation, 1989):

> *"To come to Medjugorje means to rediscover the Bible, to start to live the Bible and to listen well to what it reveals, what this Divine Word has done in the heart and in the life of Our Lady. The embodiment of the New Testament, the Words of Our Lord, is always current, always alive. The Word of God with that same power and strength is waiting for your fiat, just as Mary gave hers."*

And Father Jozo added:
> *"...Medjugorje is a sign for our times, our generation, that our generation becomes what God wants—and this is the Church, the seed, the light, the teacher, the mother, peace, salvation for all, prophet to all, priest and preacher to all.*

Therefore, Mary's message at Medjugorje, and throughout the world, is not just a call for us to allow God to dwell in us individually; but also a call to allow God to live in the world, to live His fullest among His people.

According to Mary's messages, the Virgin chose Medjugorje as an example of how each village, town, state and nation should come to live. Thus, as she did at Fatima, Mary has come to bring Medjugorje to the world and the world to Medjugorje.

Visionary Vicka Ivankovic explained Mary's mission at Medjugorje in the book *Queen of the Cosmos* by Janice T. Connell:

> *"She wants everyone in the whole world to be saved, to live in God's loving presence. She has come to call all people in the world to listen to her messages and convert. It is dangerous to live in sin. Terrible catastrophes await those who do not turn back to God. But He always forgives us, no matter what the sin. All we have to do is ask. The Blessed Mother is calling us to ask His forgiveness now. She reminds us that God never refuses forgiveness to any of His children who ask."*

At Medjugorje in 1981, Mary announced she had come as the **"Queen of Peace,"** a title which proclaimed to the world the purpose of her mission. But Marian followers say it was also to announce that God would now fulfill His promise at Fatima of an Era of Peace and that mankind is invited to help secure this peace. And unlike previous attempts at peace over the centuries, Mary's words at Fatima indicate that God is speaking of a true peace, a peace not just between men, but between God and His people.

Mary also brought at Medjugorje the formula for this peace, so that, as she said on August 25, 1991, **"The secrets I began in Fatima may be fulfilled."** These secrets undoubtedly involve the Triumph of her Immaculate Heart and the Era of Peace as foretold at Fatima. On August 25, 1994, Mary again echoed this promise, *"I pray and intercede before My Son, Jesus, so that the dream your fathers had may be fulfilled."*

According to Sister Emmanuel Maillard, a member of the Community of the Beatitudes living in Medjugorje and author of the book *Medjugorje, the War Day by Day*, visionary Ivan Dragicevic, revealed a similar understanding. Sister Emmanuel wrote in her newsletter, *The Medjugorje Network* (April 1, 1994):

> "On this occasion (March 10, 1994), many of the visionaries were asked about the Triumph of the Immaculate Heart of Mary. Ivan said that Gospa often spoke about this, but that he could not speak about it. Mirjana also did not wish to say anything. I do not know if this will be a part of the secrets or not, but it is evident that these visionaries have received instructions from Gospa to remain silent about this…"

Many books suggest the fulfillment of the ten secrets at Medjugorje will bring about the Era of Peace with all its promises. And this Era of Peace is to be totally different from anything the world has ever known. Father John M. Lozano, a highly respected theologian and mariologist, in his book *Mary, Model of Disciples* (Claretian Publications, 1984), writes about the profound meaning of what Mary promised at Fatima,

> *"In the last century, the devotion to the Immaculate Heart was associated with the final salvation of individuals. At Fatima, too, the salvation of the individuals was mentioned, but together with the common salvation of the human race and of the Church on earth.*
>
> *"If we consecrate ourselves to Mary's Heart, there will be peace, and the chastisements of hunger, wars and persecution will cease. Note that the term peace, as contrasted with the three chastisements mentioned in the apparitions, takes on*

> *the full, Biblical sense of shalom: 'a state of well-being in communion with God and with our brothers and sisters, in which the presence of God shines through in a harmonious existence worthy of the sons and daughters of God.' Today's apparitions appear to continue to reemphasize this new perspective given at Fatima. Contemporary visionaries throughout the world cite Mary's calls for prayer and conversion, but also speak of God's coming Triumph and an Era of Peace."*

At Medjugorje, where the number of apparitions are difficult for some in the Church to comprehend, Mary's extended presence is said to be the only way she can accomplish her Fatima mission—to bring true peace into the hearts of men and the world. And while the salvation of souls is certainly the primary purpose of her mission, Mary continually notes her desire to help her children find peace on earth.

As she explained at Medjugorje in a message on May 25, 1987:

> *"I call on each one of you to consciously decide for God and against Satan. I am your Mother and, therefore, I want to lead you all to complete holiness. I want each one of you to be happy here on earth and to be with me in Heaven. That is, dear children, the purpose of my coming here, and it's my desire."*

The Virgin appears to have also confirmed at Medjugorje the type of peace Father John Lozano cited as being the message proclaimed at Fatima: the peace of God on earth, a peace among men and with God:

> *"If you would abandon yourselves to me, you will not even feel the passage from this life to the next life. You will begin to live the life of Heaven from this earth."* (1986)

Chapter Nine

TIME FOR TRUTH, TIME FOR ACTION

With the 1984 consecration of the world to the Immaculate Heart of Mary by the Holy Father and the Bishops, the final acts were set in motion for the fulfillment of the promise at Fatima of an Era of Peace. And since 1984, the rapid changes in the world, especially the fall of communism, seem to indicate that God is now acting decisively through Mary's intercession.

According to Denis Nolan, in his book, *Medjugorje! A Time for Truth, a Time for Action*, Sister Lucia of Fatima noted this in an interview on February 19, 1990:

> *"I agree perfectly with what the Holy Father said about the most recent events in the East and in Russia. I believe that it has to do with the intervention of God to free the world from the danger of a NUCLEAR WAR, which could destroy the world; and with an appeal, an urgent appeal to humanity, to live out a living faith, trustful hope and active love of God and neighbor in respect for the dignity, the rights and the life of the human person under observance of the Divine Commandments."*

But while the rapid changes are astonishing, the world is still a dangerous place. This then brings us to an important question: When will the Era of Peace begin?

Obviously, no one knows the exact time. But almost all agree what is needed most now is more prayer and conversion to help hasten the arrival of this promised period of peace.

At Medjugorje, the Virgin Mary's call to conversion has been unprecedented. Like a patient mother, Mary has gone to great lengths to explain how the world can find peace. Janice T. Connell, in the *Queen of Peace Newsletter* (Pittsburgh Center for Peace), explains:

> *"The Blessed Virgin said,* **'Peace in the world is in a state of crisis.'** *She continually invites us to reconciliation and conversion.*
>
> *"This time, this period of grace is urgent. After the visible sign, those still living will have little time for conversion. For that reason, the Blessed Virgin invites us to urgent reconciliation and conversion. The Medjugorje message contains five elements:*

Conversion to God:

"He is our Creator and Lord; hence, we must accept Him as the undisputed number one priority in our lives. Accordingly, we are to renounce our sinful ways and aim constantly at God's love and service. To this end Our Lady urges Catholics to go to Confession at least once a month.

Faith:

"Faith needs to be deep, strong, total, unhesitating, big-hearted. Nothing pleases Her more, the Madonna of Medjugorje has told us, than **to hear us reciting her favorite prayer, the Creed (that is the formula of faith).**

Prayer:

"All of us are exhorted to pray more and better, in other words, we should not only devote more time to our prayers but say them more meaningfully and devoutly; or as the Virgin puts it, we should **"pray with our heart."** She likewise stresses the value of Scripture reading, and group prayer, especially that which centers on the Mass and Eucharistic devotions. And everyone (this applies especially to priests) is encouraged to pray the Rosary.

Peace:

"Peace follows from the preceding elements as gift and reward. So central indeed is peace to her Medjugorje message that Our Lady wants June 25 (the date of her first apparition in 1981 to the definitive six-strong group) to be dedicated to herself as **'Queen of Peace'.**

"Peace, she teaches us, goes hand in hand with reconciliation. It must be with God first and foremost, leading to peace of conscience and peace with the interior world of self. Peace, the carrier and agent of reconciliation, must reach out to the world around us—all the way to every level of national life and to the war-threatened international order itself.

Fasting:

"The Mother of God reminds us that all penance and mortification (reparation) are sanctifying and draw special favors from God. She specifically invites us to fast twice a week (Wednesday's and Friday's are conventional for this)."

Thus, Mary's call at Medjugorje is not a new one. It is a call she made at Fatima and throughout the centuries. But at Fatima, it appears Mary's call was also a warning and a solution to a specific danger, a danger she revealed, through words and visions, that had to be **"prevented"** for her Triumph to come. In fact, to a great extent, her direct intercession to save the world from this specific danger will *be* her *"Triumph"*.

And, in order for God's *Triumph* to come, the faithful must now respond to Mary's call for action. It is the same call to conversion and prayer as Scripture, but contains the mystery of the *"urgency."* And without a doubt, this urgency surrounds the remaining Fatima prophecy of the *"annihilation of nations."* Thus, before the Era of Peace will arrive, Mary is telling us this dangerous prophecy must first be "reckoned with."

And at Fatima, Our Lady gave a specific formula for the faithful to help her to do just that.

Chapter Ten

"TO PREVENT THIS..."

"An atheist Russia will spread her errors throughout the world fomenting wars and great persecution of the Church. The good will be martyred and the Holy Father will have much to suffer and several entire nations will be annihilated..."
(The Virgin Mary at Fatima, July 13, 1917).

Over the decades, this ominous prophecy from Fatima has stirred the minds of many people. But Mary didn't finish with these words. Rather, she offered the world a solution: *"To prevent this, I shall come to ask for the consecration of Russia to my Immaculate Heart and the Communion of reparation on the First Saturdays."*

On May 13, 1982, Pope John Paul II made the Act of Consecration at Fatima. The following day, Sister Lucia, the lone surviving Fatima visionary, made a startling statement. She said, *"The consecration will have its effect but now to obtain world peace the apostles of Fatima will have much to do."* And Sister Lucia noted, *"There has been a tidal wave of evil and a proliferation of nuclear weapons. If we are now to avoid nuclear war, "The Blue Army will have much to do"* (Source: *Her Own Words to the Nuclear Age* by John Haffert)

To affect the changes in Russia, it was apparently necessary for the Holy Father to again consecrate the world in 1984 to the Immaculate Heart of Mary, collegially with all the Bishops. This, almost all Fatima experts agree, began the conversion of Russia. But many say Russia's full conversion is incomplete for a reason.

According to John Haffert, one of the founders of the World

Apostolate of Fatima (The Blue Army), *"'Conversion' means a 'turning around'. And spiritually, the big turn around in Russia was from militant atheism to theism. It was from illegality of religion to legality. It was from suppression and persecution to legalization and support.* And this is specifically what Mary meant, according to Haffert, when she spoke of the **'*conversion*'** of Russia. She and Jesus, in different colloquies with Sr. Lucia, used interchangeably the expressions **"*conversion of Russia*"** and **"End persecution in that nation."**

Sister Lucia, in an interview conducted on October 11, 1992, concurred with this opinion. Lucia noted the conversion of Russia has begun and that Our Lady never meant Russia would be converted to Catholicism. Said Lucia, *"The fact is that in Russia the Communist, atheist power prevented the people from carrying out their faith. People now have an individual choice..."* (Source: *Her Own Words* by John Haffert)

But according to Haffert and other Fatima experts, Russia is not fully converted and the one remaining "warning" from Our Lady at Fatima that has not been fulfilled, **"Several entire nations will be annihilated,"** is still looming over mankind like a storm cloud that will not go away. Indeed, it is still present, even though the conversion of Russia has begun. And Fatima experts say we can discern from Mary's words, and the "two" great miracles foretold at Fatima (the October 13th, 1917 miracle of the sun and the January 25-26, 1938 "great sign" or "illumination" of the sky over much of Europe), what exactly this "danger" is.

At Fatima on October 13, 1917, during the miracle of the sun, almost everyone within a radius of several miles believed they were about to be consumed by fire. They thought the ball of fire crashing down upon them was actually the sun. Most believed it was the end of the world.

In 1938, it happened again. On the evening of January 25th, a great illumination over the northern hemisphere had people running into the streets in terror. Some thought, like in 1917, it was the end of the world. At the time, scientists said it was an aurora borealis. But Sister Lucia, at her convent in Spain, said "*no*". It was the "*great sign*", she insisted, God promised in 1917.

Writes John Haffert, in his book, To Prevent This, "*Why would a merciful mother terrorize her children with fire? Why would she have done this unless it were like a warning of what can happen if the world does not respond to the message of hope God has sent to deliver us?*"

In 1917, Mary's prophecy that **"various nations will be annihilated"** caused both wonder and astonishment. Since there would not be another deluge, in what other way could entire nations be '*annihilated*' (which means wiped out, made into nothing)? But that was before mankind knew of the atomic bomb.

Haffert explains, "*Then in 1945, it happened. Two cities were wiped out by the first simple atomic bombs. And it is noteworthy that in the very announcement to the world of that 'annihilation', the President of the United States said: 'Man has learned to harness the power of the sun.' And at Fatima, tens of thousands of people thought it was the sun itself falling upon them.*"

Curiously, some scientists now say the 1938 "*illumination*" was not an aurora borealis. But rather, it appears to be a light of an unknown origin that is similar to what would occur with *a "massive nuclear detonation."*

It cannot be overemphasized that on October 13, 1973, the anniversary of the miracle of the sun which Our Lady performed at Fatima **"so that all may believe"**, Mary appeared in Akita, Japan and said,

> **"If men do not repent and better themselves, the Father will inflict a terrible punishment on all humanity. It will be a punishment greater than the deluge...Fire will fall from the sky and will wipe out a**

> *great part of humanity...I alone can still save you from the calamities which approach."* (Two months before, on August 6, 1973, the anniversary date of the atomic bombing of Hiroshima, Mary warned Sister Agnes of *"a great chastisement for all mankind."*)

Unlike Mary's message at Fatima in 1917, this prophecy speaks in almost biblical language. For no evil comes from God, but only from sin. But God, seeing the pride and wickedness which had come into the world leading to one global war after another, permitted man to do what President Truman described: *"harness the power of the sun"*, a power, which just touching the earth, can scorch and destroy.

During the Cuban missile crisis, Secretary Robert McNamara, who spent the entire twelve days of the crisis in the Pentagon (day and night), kept saying that when we face such a crisis now, we must realize that we are talking about *"the death not of thousands, or even millions, but of nations."*

At Fatima, Mary said: **"Several entire nations will be annihilated."** At Akita, Our Lady said: **"Fire will fall from the sky and will wipe out a great part of humanity."** To Sr. Lucia, in March of 1939, Jesus said, **"Ask, ask insistently for the promulgation of the Communion of Reparation on the First Saturdays, the time is coming when the rigor of My justice will punish the crimes of various nations. Some of them will be annihilated."**

According to Haffert, *"In addition to all the reasons above, it appears to many that the warning given at Akita ("fire from the sky will wipe out a great part of humanity") is the same as that of Fatima ("several entire nations will be annihilated"). The Bishop of Akita who issued the pastoral letter himself was of this opinion."*

And Bishop Ito indeed, made it clear as to when he believed God would act, *"It seems to me that Our Heavenly Father needs to purify this corrupt world before allowing mankind to enter the 21st century."*

Chapter Eleven

"THE FRUIT OF ABORTION IS NUCLEAR WAR"

Today, Mary keeps warning visionaries that this specific danger, the danger of a nuclear *"annihilation of nations"*, is still alive. It is a danger that could destroy the world even though the fall of communism and the conversion of Russian has begun.

And Our Lady says, with mankind's all out attack on life through abortion, contraception, and euthanasia, these sins are drawing the world closer to danger. Indeed, Mother Teresa of Calcutta's words ring loud and clear, *"The fruit of abortion is nuclear war."* This reality was echoed by Pope John Paul in his October, 1987 visit to America when he said, *"The very condition of your survival as a nation depends on how you treat the weakest among you-those yet unborn in the womb."* Likewise, the Virgin Mary told Father Stefano Gobbi on December 31, 1994:

> *"I am a sorrowful Mother, as I see this poor humanity, so far away from its Lord, a humanity which, with great irresponsibility and indifference, is walking alone the road of sin and evil, of impurity and godlessness, of hatred and war.*
>
> *How great is the danger of humanity reaching the point of destroying itself by its own hands! I see your roads bathed with blood, while violence and hatred hurl themselves like a terrible hurricane upon the life of families and nations."*

And on August 3, 1996, the Virgin told Estela Ruiz of Phoenix Arizona,

> *"How I have prayed for all of your souls. How I have prayed that all be converted to God's goodness and love. It has been my desire that all of my earthly children would turn to God, to His saving grace. Yet, in all this time I have been in the world, letting you know of God's love for you, of my Son's passionate sacrifice for you and of the power of God's Holy Spirit, there are many who do not believe and because of this lack of faith are helping to move this world to devastation. I have come to call you, all of you in the world. Many have listened, many have not. If your world is to be saved from devastation, it must turn to God and His tender love..."*
>
> *"It is evident that your world is moving towards devastation more and more each day. As terrorism, hatred for each other, acts of violence increase in every corner of the world, no one can deny that something is horribly wrong. It is becoming more and more visible that there is a destructive force moving over the earth and it is also very visible that we are nearing the peak of hatred and destruction.*
>
> *"How long will my children of the world continue to be blind to the increase in intolerance of each other? How far will you, all of my earthly children, let it go — until it is too late to turn back?"*

According to some Marian authorities, we now need to place close attention to Our Lady's request for the Communion of Reparation of First Saturdays and to the words of Our Lord to Sister Lucia in 1939 when He too said, **"ask insistently for the Communion of Reparation."** For if the consecration of Russia by the Holy Father and the Bishops in 1984 is accepted, as Sister Lucia says it has, it is only through this second request of Our Lady of Fatima that the world will truly find peace and escape annihilation.

Dr. Rosalie Turton of the 101 Foundation agrees. She insists we must urgently focus on Mary's call at Fatima for reparation. Says Dr. Turton, *"The vision Sister Lucia received in 1929 confirms the importance of the request for the Communion of Reparation of First Saturdays."* In 1929, Our Lady said to Sister Lucia, **"The moment has come for God to ask the Holy Father, in union with the Bishops of the world, to make the consecration of Russia to My Immaculate Heart. He promises to save Russia by this means."** *However, in letters written by Sister Lucia in the 1930's, Lucia makes it clear that the reparation to the Immaculate Heart of Mary is necessary. The practice of reparation is ultimately intended to bring about true conversion of Russia through the collegial consecration. The delay in accomplishing the full conversion of Russia is related to insufficient reparation."*

Indeed, this makes sense and is in keeping with Pope Pius XI's encyclical, *Miserentissimus Redemptor*, which spoke of how consecration and reparation must go hand in hand. Wrote Pope Pius XI,

> *"Whereas the primary object of consecration is that the creature should repay the love of the Creator by loving Him in return, yet from this another naturally follows - that is to make amends for the insults offered to the Divine Love by oblivion and neglect, and by the sins and offenses of mankind. This duty is commonly called by the name of reparation."*

At Fatima, in 1916, a year before Mary first appeared, an

angel came to the children and taught them this prayer of reparation,

> *O most Holy Trinity, Father, Son and Holy Spirit, I adore Thee profoundly. I offer Thee the most precious Body, blood, soul and Divinity of Jesus Christ, present in all the tabernacles of the world, in reparation for the outrages, sacrileges of the world and indifference by which He is offended. By the infinite merits of the Sacred Heart of Jesus and the Immaculate Heart of Mary, I beg the conversion of poor sinners.*

What kind of reparation did the Virgin request at Fatima? Mary asked for people to:

1) *PRAY THE ROSARY*
2) *WEAR THE SCAPULAR*
3) *MAKE THE COMMUNION OF REPARATION OF THE FIRST SATURDAY OF EACH MONTH. THIS INCLUDES CONFESSION, COMMUNION, ROSARY, AND TO SPEND AT LEAST 15 MINUTES IN MEDITATION UPON THE MYSTERIES OF THE ROSARY*

At Fatima in 1917, and again at Medjugorje in 1991, Mary promised the **"Triumph of her Immaculate Heart"**. These are words which few believe can be truly meaningful if the world is reduced to a burning ash. Indeed, there must be hope. And there, must be action, the same kind of action that occurred at Lepanto and during other great crises of the Church!

Indeed, the primary action Mary requests in order to fulfill the urgent need for reparation is for the faithful to pray and meditate upon the Rosary. Thus, the Queen of Peace is again saying ***"The Rosary can save the world!"***

"I believe the chastisement can still be prevented," asserted John Haffert at the 1996 Lay Apostolate Foundation's retreat in Washington, New Jersey. Haffert's confidence in God, comes from more than just his belief that Mary's Triumph cannot be called such if a great part of humanity is annihilated. Rather, he explicitly notes how the sun, during the great miracle of October 13, 1917 at Fatima, returned to its position in the sky at the last moment when thousands believed it was about to strike the earth. Thus, Haffert argues this was a sign that some day, at a decisive moment, God will spare His people from a great suffering.

And many believe that some day is approaching fast!

This appears to be what Mary is also saying: Her victory is near and will come. And like centuries before, it will come through her direct intercession. But, what still needs to be done is a great amount of prayer, along with consistent and generous acts of reparation by God's people. Thus, it appears that Our Lady is in need of a great outpouring of Rosaries.

For it is through the Rosary, Mary exhorts, that she will bring the world into the ***"Era of Peace"***. And it is through the Rosary, she unequivocally emphasizes, that she can ***"prevent"*** the ***"annihilation of nations"***. Therefore, both of Fatima's remaining prophecies can be understood to be inescapably tied to the Rosary!

Indeed, Mary appeared at Fatima on October 13, 1917 with the Rosary in her hand and announced to the children that she was ***"The Lady of the Rosary."*** It was an announcement that can be seen today as more than just a declaration of her title and identity to the children.

Rather, as at Lourdes, it had everything to do with why she had come to Fatima and what she was trying to desperately tell the world to do...before it is too late!

Chapter Twelve

"OUR LADY DOES NOT WANT NUCLEAR WAR"

From Our Lady's revelations, it appears she is referring to not just the overall change that God will bring into the world through her Triumph, but also to a great individual victory, much like at Lepanto in 1571.

This victory will be marked by a decisive moment. It is a moment, Mary's messages indicate, in which she will snatch victory from the jaws of defeat, leaving Satan crushed, as foretold in Genesis.

Indeed, this is what St. John Bosco foretold in a prophecy. The 19th century saint saw an epic battle between the forces of good and evil around the year 2,000 A.D., culminating in a great victory for the Church through Mary.

It is to be a victory of the importance of Lepanto, St. Bosco indicated. In fact, his prophecy was so well known, a church in his hometown of Turin immortalized it in stone, first by recalling Lepanto and then foretelling Mary's future Triumph in a year approaching the third millennium.

On October 13, 1917, Mary confirmed at Fatima the approaching fulfillment of this prophecy. Thirteen years later the Church also did so in its approval of Fatima.

Most significantly, two great signs were given at Fatima to solidify the truth of the Virgin's words. But it appears these two signs not only reveal the nature of the threat that would begin in 1945, but perhaps also the specific manner in which the Virgin Mary will *"triumph"*. For time and time again, especially in the second half of the twentieth century, we find indicators Mary has come and is actively interceding through the prayers of her little ones **"to prevent"** the world from destroying itself through a nuclear engagement.

As Father Slavko Barbaric of Medjugorje stated in Michael Brown's book, *The Final Hour*, the hand writing is on the wall as to what Mary is trying to accomplish. Says Father Barbaric:

> *"The Madonna did not come to announce catastrophes, but more to help us avoid them. We all know nuclear war is possible, even without apparitions. If a house burns, it doesn't burn because the mother cries "fire". On the contrary, the mother comes to save the house which is burning and in that there is hope."*

Indeed, right from the start of the nuclear age in August, 1945, we see Mary's hand at work. The four Jesuit priests who survived at Hiroshima, Fathers Lasalle, Kleinsorge, Cieslik, and Schiffer were at the very epicenter of the atomic bomb explosion. Yet they were not harmed. Immediately afterward, these priests declared it was the Fatima prayers, especially the Rosary, which saved them. The same thing occurred at Nagasaki, where the Fatima prayers reportedly preserved the lives of a group of friars who were at ground zero of the atomic blast and survived without any radiation effects.

Eleven days after the bombing, on August 15th, the Feast of Mary's Assumption, World War II officially ended. Remarkably, the church the priests had survived in was the Jesuit Church of Our Lady's Assumption. Thus, the presence of Mary's hand at work is evident. But more would quickly follow.

For some unknown reason, on May 13, 1955, the Soviet Union packed up and departed Austria, the crown jewel and strategic centerpiece of its post - WWII European occupation. This occurred after 70,000 Austrians agreed to pray what Mary asked for at Fatima: the Rosary! The May 13th, departure date of the Russians, the anniversary of the first apparition at Fatima, speaks again for itself in meaning and significance.

Then, on October 12-13, 1960 another major intercession by Mary is recognized to have possibly prevented the world from experiencing nuclear destruction. Father Albert Shamon, in his book *The Power of the Rosary*, relays this amazing story:

> "Most of us remember the time when Nikita Khrushchev visited the United Nations in October, 1960 and boasted that "they would bury us" —would annihilate us! And to emphasize his boasting, he took off his shoe and pounded the desk before the horrified world assembly.
>
> "This was no idle boast. Khrushchev knew his scientists had been working on a nuclear missile and had completed their work and planned in November 1960, the 43rd anniversary of the Bolshevik Revolution, to present it to Khrushchev.
>
> "But here's what happened. Pope John XXIII had opened and read the Third Fatima Secret given to Sister Lucy. He authorized the Bishop of Leiria (Fatima) to write to all the bishops of the world, inviting them to join with the pilgrims of Fatima on the night of October 12-13, 1960, in prayer and penance for Russia's conversion and consequent world peace.
>
> "On the night of October 12-13, about a million pilgrims spent the night outdoors in the Cova da Iria at Fatima in prayer and penance before the Blessed Sacrament. They prayed and watched despite a penetrating rain which chilled them to the bone.
>
> "At the same time at least 300 dioceses throughout the world joined with them. Pope John XXIII sent a special blessing to all taking part in this unprecedented night of reparation.
>
> "On the night between October 12 and 13, right after his shoe-pounding episode, Khrushchev suddenly pulled up stakes and enplaned in all haste for Moscow, cancelling all

subsequent engagements. Why?

"Marshall Nedelin, the best minds in Russia on nuclear energy and several government officials were present for the final testing of the missile that was going to be presented to Khrushchev. When countdown was completed, the missile, for some reason or other, did not leave the launch pad. After 15 or 20 minutes, Nedelin and all others came out of the shelter. When they did, the missile exploded killing over 300 people. This set back Russia's nuclear program for 20 years, prevented all-out atomic warfare, the burying of the U.S.- and this happened on the night when the whole Catholic world was on its knees before the Blessed Sacrament, gathered at the feet of our Rosary Queen in Fatima. OUR LADY DOES NOT WANT NUCLEAR WAR!"

Indeed, Mary does not want nuclear proliferation of any kind. And in order to once again convey this message, one of the most incredible miracles occurred during the French testing of an atomic bomb in the Pacific in 1968.

From pictures taken of the explosion by a photographer, it can be clearly seen in the center of the atomic mushroom cloud the undeniable image of Our Lord crucified on the cross.

And to the right of Christ, an image of Our Lady is seen glowing in an all- white silhouette. This radiating image of Mary is distinctly visible in contrast against the background of the red mushroom cloud. It even appears to be the same likeness as *Our Lady of Medjugorje!*

Both *Newsweek* and *U.S. News* and *World Report* magazines ran the photograph in the summer of 1989, with the latter disclosing a *"secret"* plan in the event of nuclear war. This being an irony not lost upon those who have pondered the contents of the previously unrevealed Third Secret of Fatima.

Still, the message behind the miraculous photograph is clear! Our Lady does not want nuclear war!

Chapter Thirteen

REAGAN, GORBACHEV AND THE VIRGIN MARY

Over and over, it appears Mary has come specifically to prevent nuclear *"annihilation."* For the *"Fatima - Nuclear connection"* over the decades repeatedly shows its face.

From the October 1962 Cuban missile crisis, to the 1964 defeat of communism in Brazil, to the visionary Sister Agnes Sassagawa of the Akita, Japan apparitions taking her vows in Nagasaki, there are brief and corollary signs that reinforce Mary's visible role in interceding to disarm nuclear tension.

But beginning in the 1980's, Mary's intercessions *"to prevent"* the world from destroying itself and to bring the peace promised at Fatima becomes even more evident. As if in fulfillment of her words at Medjugorje, which announce she has come to *"fulfill the Secrets I began in Fatima,"* Mary's hand can be found in great world events.

Fr. Luigi Bianchi, a well known Mariologist and authority on Fatima, concludes that Our Lady has come to fulfill her promises at Fatima. In his book, *Fatima and Medjugorje*, Fr. Bianchi writes,

> *"The message of Medjugorje is a continuation and a complement of the message of Fatima. It is the extraordinary verification of it in substance. It is the same message of peace for this century of the most dreadful wars in history and of the menace of a fiery deluge of an atomic apocalypse. Fatima happened in 1917 towards the end of the First World War. Medjugorje is happening between the Second*

> World War and the dawning of the third millennium. The Mother of God guides us toward the door of peace.
> "The first words of Fatima and of Medjugorje are those of the Annunciation: '**Do not be afraid' (Luke 1:30)**.
> "The messages are illustrated, attested to and confirmed by signs in the sky, which have happened at both Fatima and Medjugorje.
> "Why this new message at Medjugorje? Because those of the Cova de Iria had not been listened to and remain not understood."

Most significantly, we apparently do not understand how close the world has repeatedly come, as Fr. Bianchi states, "*to an atomic apocalypse.*"

On May 13, 1984, as one of the greatest crowds ever to come to Fatima celebrated the anniversary of the Virgin's first apparition there by praying the Rosary, another significant event occurred that would again help **"to prevent"** nuclear conflict.

On that day, a massive explosion eliminated two-thirds of the surface to air and ship to ship missiles of the Soviet Union's most powerful fleet, the Northern Fleet.

According to *Jane's Defense Weekly* of London, this was "*the greatest disaster to occur in the Soviet navy since WW II*" Could this have been an accident of great significance? According to Sister Lucia, "*a nuclear war would have occurred in 1985.*" (Source: *The Triumphant Queen of the World*, 1995 by Daniel J. Lynch)

Four years later, it happened again! As thousands prayed all night long on May 12, 1988, during the vigil of the anniversary of the apparitions at Fatima, another major explosion shut down the Soviet Union's sole missile motor plant. The Associated Press reported at the time, "*A major explosion has shut down the only plant in the Soviet Union that makes the main rocket motors of that country's newest long-range nuclear missile, according to U.S. officials."* The Pentagon released a statement noting the accident occurred on May 12th and *"destroyed several buildings at a Soviet propellant plant in Paulogriad."*

Curiously, just a week before, on May 3, 1988, a similar eruption ripped apart a Nevada facility believed to be handling the ammonium perchlorate used in the main rocket motor for the SS-24.

Indeed, the *"signs"* of the Virgin's Mary's timely intercessions are considerable and well documented, as she repeatedly leaves evidence which tie the events in our lives to her words at Fatima.

But after the 1984 consecration of the world by Pope John Paul II, a string of events beginning with the rise of President Gorbachev in the Soviet Union especially reveal Mary's intercessions to **"prevent annihilation,"** and to convert Russia.

Gorbachev's policies of *"perestroika"* and *"glasnost"* were soon implemented setting the stage for the great world events to come. Indeed, on July 3, 1987, in speaking about the Triumph of the Immaculate Heart to Fr. Stefano Gobbi, the Virgin Mary revealed, **"These times are closer than you think. Already, during this Marian Year, certain great events will take place, concerning what I predicted at Fatima and have told, under secrecy, to the children to whom I am appearing at Medjugorje."**

Five months later, world events confirmed Mary's words. Soviet President Gorbachev came to the United States and signed the *Peace Accord*. It was December 8th, the Feast of the Immaculate Conception!

Just prior to signing the accord, President Ronald Reagan was given by Alfred Kingon, America's Ambassador to Europe, a letter from Marija Pavlovic, one of the visionaries in Medjugorje. According to Kingon, President Reagan, visibly moved, phoned his thanks to Marija in Medjugorje, and then proceeded to his meeting with Gorbachev after first exclaiming, *"Now I am going to this meeting with a new spirit!"*

At the request of Ambassador Kingon, Marija Pavlovic would later write President Gorbachev. According to Kingon, this message was translated into Russian and put directly into the hands of Gorbachev at the Kremlin!. As Maria Pavlovic had with President Reagan, she informed Gorbachev of Mary's message of peace, a message that Mary fortified at Medjugorje in 1983 by asking for people to now pray **"all fifteen decades of the Rosary"** each day.

Sometime later, President Reagan wrote Fr. Juan Villanova, Chaplain of the Sanctuary of Fatima, Portugal, thanking him for having sent the Pilgrim Statue of Our Lady of Fatima. It was, said Reagan, *"upstairs in Nancy's and my bedroom"* at the White House when he and Soviet President Mikhail Gorbachev *"were meeting downstairs!"*

A non-Catholic, Ambassador Kingon served as a Secretary to President Reagan's Cabinet before being appointed Ambassador to Europe. At the 1992 National Conference on Medjugorje at Notre Dame, Kingon gave his own testimony as to the authenticity of Mary's apparitions. Said Kingon, *"Our Lady is now coming for all her children on earth, in preparation for a major turning point in the affairs of men!"*

But probably the most compelling heavenly intercession to preserve world peace came in 1991, when *EIGHT* hard-line Communists in the Soviet Union attempted to overthrow President Gorbachev by kidnapping him and placing him under house arrest.

The attempted coup was denounced and defeated, and consequently the Communists were not permitted to regain power in Russia. However, while the actual facts surrounding this historical event are well documented, so also is Mary's powerful intercession to prevent disaster.

In 1987, the Virgin Mary appeared at Hrushiv in the Ukraine to a long time Catholic underground dissident named Josyp Terelya. With a Rosary in her right hand and the Christ Child in her left, Mary gave Josyp messages which foretold the future. Two years later, in 1989, Terelya received a powerful dream which described and predicted almost to the letter the coming (1991) coup against Gorbachev.

Writes Terelya and Michael Brown in their book, *Witness*:

> *"I saw a map of the Ukraine and the bloody river began to dry up. The earth in many places was scorched and took on a black-gray color. This was the color of death. But amid the black-gray ashes I saw grass sprouting. It was very tall. I saw the people kneeling and crying but I knew these were the tears of joy and salvation. I saw the new Babylon, the red city, that was falling into the earth. In that city, under a Christian temple, was a secret hiding place. There were EIGHT men there—eight rulers, all eight waxen yellow. They laughed horribly and bared their teeth. Gorbachev told me it wasn't he who was in charge of the state. I saw the real leader of the USSR behind a yellow screen: It was Lucifer himself."*

And Satan, as God would reveal, was intent on pushing the world to the brink of disaster!

Chapter Fourteen

THE QUEEN OF PEACE

While the secular press acknowledged the great danger to world peace the Soviet coup presented, God not only foretold the event to Josyp Terelya, but afterwards confirmed it's significance.

Around the time of the Gorbachev crisis, the Virgin Mary's messages at Medjugorje (August and September 1991) and her message to Father Stefano Gobbi (September 1991) directly invoked both the reminder of her promised *Triumph* at Fatima and that this Triumph is related to the *"prevention of annihilation."*

On August 25, 1991, just three days after the end of the attempted coup in the Soviet Union, Mary announced for the first time at Medjugorje that she would **"fulfill"** the **"secrets I began in Fatima"** One month later, again for the first time at Medjugorje, the Virgin called for **"the Triumph of my Immaculate Heart."** These messages clearly echo Fatima's announcement of victory, a victory that will save the world from **"annihilation,"** as once again threatened in the August coup attempt.

Likewise, the Virgin told Father Stefano Gobbi in Slovakia on September 12, 1991, less than one month after the attempted coup in the Soviet Union, that it was her direct intercession that brought the collapse of communism. And with the recent failure of the coup, Mary's message insinuated that, indeed, communism was defeated,

"This is my Work alone and I myself am furthering it in every part of the world. Because these are the

times of my Triumph, of my victory and of your salvation.

"-In the name of your heavenly Mother, yes in the Name of Mary, the Turks were defeated, when they laid siege to the city of Vienna and threatened to invade and destroy the whole Christian world. They were far superior in strength, in numbers and in weapons, and they felt that their victory was assured. But I was publicly invoked and called upon; my name was inscribed upon their banners and shouted out by the soldiers and thus, through my intercession, there took place the miracle of this victory which saved the Christian world from its destruction. It is for this reason that the Pope instituted, on this day, the Feast of the Name of Mary.

"In the Name of Mary, Marxist communism, which for decades had been exercising its rule and holding so many of my poor children in oppressive and bloody slavery, has been defeated in these countries. Not because of political movements or persons, but through my personal intervention, has your liberation finally come about." (September 12, 1991)

From the Virgin Mary's messages surrounding the August, 1991, failed coup in the former USSR, it is evident that God wishes us to know the outcome of the events were arranged and controlled by Him. Through Mary's intercession, the entire affair was one of a miraculous nature.

Curiously, just *one* month before the coup in July, 1991, *Life Magazine* boldly presented on its cover a picture of a statue of the Virgin Mary that stands in the front of St. James Church in Medjugorje. The cover of *Life* read, *"Do you Believe in Miracles?,"* words which easily can be interpreted to find their profound meaning in the amazingly peaceful collapse of the Soviet Union, and again in the swift and decisive failure of the attempted coup.

Chapter Fifteen

THE LAST CRUSADE

God's desire for us to recognize His hand in the affairs of men is fascinating. By repeatedly showing us how significant world events somehow land on Church feast days, mankind has been given a series of *signs* from heaven to illuminate and confirm God's presence in our everyday lives. This is a phenomena especially found in the 20th century.

Most importantly, with Mary's announcement at Fatima that God wished to establish in the world greater devotion to the Immaculate Heart of Mary, the dates of critical events linked to the prophecies of Fatima have not only been repeatedly found on Church Feast days, but especially Marian Feast days.

World War II is generally recognized to have truly become a world war on December 8, 1941, the Feast of the Immaculate Conception. This was the day the United States Congress declared war on Japan and Germany. After this, many critical events in the war landed on Marian Feasts, but it is especially noted how the A-bomb was tested at the *"Trinity Site"* in New Mexico on July 16, 1945, the Feast of Our Lady of Mt. Carmel. And how one month later, the war ended on August 15, the Feast of the Assumption of Mary.

The May 13, 1981 attempted assassination of Pope John Paul II in St. Peters square is such a well known Fatima-related event that even the secular press has not shied away from noting this "coincidence." For followers of Fatima, like the Pope himself, it was undeniable proof of the fulfillment of Mary's prophetic words, ***"The Holy Father will have much to suffer."***

The August, 1991, attempted coup in the USSR is no exception to this "date phenomena." For it was August 17, 1991, when the coup

65

began, the exact date of Mary's apparition at Fatima in August, 1917. (This was because Our Lady was unable to appear to the children on August 13, as they "too" had been imprisoned by communist authorities in Portugal.) And it was August 22, 1991 when the coup ended, the Church Feast of the Queenship of Mary. On that same day, Latvia and Estonia, both heavily Catholic, became independent nations.

The Feast of the Queenship of Mary is especially noted in regards to Fatima, for it was Pope Pius XII's 1954 encyclical that declared *"in the doctrine of Mary's Queenship lies the world's greatest hope for peace."* It is a doctrine, Fatima experts emphasize, intimately linked with Mary's promise of Her Triumph at Fatima. Pope Paul VI echoed this belief in his encyclical *Signum Magnum*, issued on the occasion of his visit to Fatima on May 13, 1967. And on May 13, 1971, the 25th anniversary of the proclamation of Pope Pius XII of Our Lady of Fatima as *"Queen of the World,"* pilgrim Virgin statues of Our Lady of Fatima were crowned throughout the world.

And there appear to be more such signs associated with the fall of communism in the USSR. Several months after the coup attempt, on Christmas Day, December 25, 1991, Gorbachev resigned as president of the Soviet Union. On January 1, 1992, the Feast day of Mary, the Holy Mother of God, Russia became an independent nation. And on September 8, 1992, the Church celebrated birthday of Mary, the last Soviet flag was brought down from aboard the Mir (Peace) spacecraft.

From all of this and Mary's messages, it is clear Our Lady is slowly winning her war with Satan. And the Virgin is winning, she says, through the power of the Rosary. It is a power that will, Mary promises, bring the final victory foretold at Fatima. This is an observation even the Wall Street Journal cited just one month after the failed coup when it stated, quoting Pope John Paul II, that *"the collapse of communism...compels us to think in a special way about Fatima."* (*Wall Street Journal*, September 27, 1991.)

Indeed, Mary's promise at Fatima of a great victory for God through the Rosary is revealed time and time again through historical events, both past and present. It was reportedly on October 13, 1886, that Pope Leo XIII, the great champion of the Rosary, received his vision of a coming showdown between Satan and God. And it was in October, 1917, when St. Maximillan Kolbe founded the Militia Immaculata, one of the greatest movements ever *"to win the world for Mary."* It would be a win, Kolbe admonished his followers, obtained by *"fingering the beads of the Rosary"*.

It was the Rosary the Jesuit priests were praying at Hiroshima that fateful day of August 6, 1945, and it was the Rosary that 70,000 people promised to pray in Austria for seven years before the Soviet's departed on May 13, 1955. Likewise, it was the Rosary that over 600,000 women in Brazil banned together to pray in 1962 in order to stymie the communist revolution in Brazil.

Since 1989, the Virgin Mary repeatedly asserts in her messages that, indeed, the Rosary is slowly but surely bringing victory. The peaceful collapse of communism in Eastern Europe, the Soviet Union, Nicaragua, El Salvador, and other Soviet satellite countries is proof, Our Lady says. As are the other relatively peaceful collapses of tyrannical dictatorships in such countries as Panama, Grenada and the Philippines.

Likewise, the end of Apartheid and the quick resolution of the Gulf War are also to be recognized as evidence, visionaries tell us, of Mary's mighty intercession for her children through their prayers, especially the prayer of the Rosary. As Mary said at Medjugorje on January 25, 1991, just days after Iraq President Saddam Hussein flooded the Persian gulf with oil, and later ignited the Kuwait oil wells on fire:

> *"Satan is strong and wishes not only to destroy human life but also nature and the planet…God sent me so that I can help you. …the Rosary alone can do miracles in the world and in lives!"*

While some would dispute the reality of these claims, they are the foolish ones. For how else than through God and prayer could the most militant, violent, and deadly reign of organized evil in the history of the world have been peacefully defeated.

Indeed, and now the Queen of Peace says the rest will follow. And it will again occur through her intercession and the power of prayer. As Mary told Father Gobbi, one month after the failed coup in the USSR,

> *"It will again be in the Name of Mary that I will bring to completion my Work with the defeat of Masonry, of every diabolical force, of materialism, and of practical atheism, so that all humanity will be able to attain its encounter with the Lord and be thus purified and completely renewed, with the Triumph of my Immaculate Heart in the world.*
>
> *"It is for this reason that I desire that the feast in honor of the Name of Mary be restored, now that you are entering into the fiercest moments of the struggle and the most painful stage of the great tribulation."*
> (September 12, 1991)

Along with Mary's requests for a feast day in honor of her name and for the declaration of her final dogma of Coredemptrix, Mediatrix and Advocate, perhaps now more than ever, a great Rosary Crusade is needed. Perhaps it will be the *Last Crusade*. It must be a crusade greater than ever before, for it will culminate with Mary securing her final victory and preventing any *"atomic"* disaster. As Our Lady told Father Gobbi on October 7, 1983, the Feast day of the Most Holy Rosary:

> *"Prayer possesses a potent force and starts a chain reaction in good that is far more powerful than any atomic reaction."*

The Virgin's words here are again carefully delivered for us to grasp what she is calling for. Indeed, there can be no doubt, Mary needs for her message at Fatima to be once again implemented in its fullest meaning by her **"children"** taking action.

And on August 3, 1996, Mary told Estela Ruiz that she needed all her **"children"** to now come together in action, before it is too late,

> *"To those of you who have heard my call I say this: if you believe that God loves you, and if you love Him, you can no longer sit still and do nothing. You must join forces and fight for the faith that you have been given... Begin now — don't wait any longer. You, my beloved, cannot wait any longer."*
> *"Say the Rosary every day"*,

Mary repeated at Fatima to the three children, **"to obtain peace for the world."** Indeed, this is what we all must now do. For the remaining prophecies of Fatima are now upon us. And soon Mary says, Satan will be chained once again in hell. Mystically chained, the Queen of Peace assures us, by the links of the Rosary.

No words could end this story better than what the Queen of Peace told Father Stefano Gobbi on October 7, 1992, the Feast of Our Lady of the Rosary,

> *"The Rosary is my prayer; it is the prayer which I came down from heaven to ask of you, because it is the weapon which you must make use of, in these times of the great battle, and it is the sign of my assured victory...*
>
> *"The chain, with which the great Dragon is to be bound, is made up of prayer made with me and by means of me. This prayer is that of the Holy Rosary..."*

Epilogue

THE TRIUMPH OF THE LORD

On the day Mary announced at Fatima she was the *"Lady of the Rosary,"* her words carried the promise of the Triumph of her Immaculate Heart and an Era of peace for the world.

While Mary's words at Fatima are understandable in their basic meaning, their exact usage is critical. For God could have announced His victory using any number of phrases or words to do so. Yet, Mary specifically said there would come the *"Triumph of her Immaculate Heart.*

And around the world today, at all of the major apparition sites, the most credible mystics and visionaries report messages that echo Fatima's announcement to the letter.

At Medjugorje, the Virgin Mary said to Maria Pavlovic,
"Therefore, dear children, help my Immaculate Heart to Triumph in the sinful world." (September 25, 1991)

In Como Italy, the Virgin Mary told Father Stefano Gobbi,
"For this, as a breaking dawn, you will as of today see my light becoming stronger and stronger, until it encircles the whole earth, ready now to open itself to the new day, which will begin with the Triumph of my Immaculate Heart in the world." (December 8, 1993)

In South Phoenix, Arizona the Virgin Mary said to Estela Ruiz,

"You will see my hand at work through world events and you will understand that the Triumph of my Immaculate Heart is near at hand." (October 31, 1992)

Thus, these messages and others throughout the world, reinforce and confirm Fatima's prophetic and monumental announcement of the coming of a great victory for God.

It is a victory, as understood by the specific words of so many visionaries, which will come through Mary's call to peace, prayer and conversion. Indeed, this victory will fulfill the prophecies of numerous visionaries and saints over the centuries such as Catherine Laboure, Mary of Agreda, Maximillan Kolbe and Louis de Montfort, all whom were devoted to Our Lady.

Most significantly, Mary's appearance at a place named Fatima, which is the name of the daughter of Mohammand, especially invokes the words of St. Louis de Montfort, when he prophesied the immense magnitude of Our Lord's coming victory through His Mother. Said the great saint,

> *"It was revealed to me that through the intercession of the Mother of God, all heresies will disappear. This victory over heresies has been reserved by Christ for His Blessed Mother. In the last times the Lord will especially spread the renown of His Mother: Mary began salvation and by her intercession it will be concluded. Before the Second Coming of Christ, Mary must, more than ever, shine in mercy, might and grace in order to bring unbelievers into the Catholic Faith. The powers of Mary in the last times over the demons will be very conspicuous. Mary will extend the Reign of Christ over the heathens and Mohammedans, and it will be a time of great joy when Mary, as Mistress and Queen of Hearts, is enthroned!"*

A FINAL NOTE

Dear Reader,

As I have tried to present in this book, I believe we are now in need of the greatest Rosary Crusade in history to secure the *"Triumph"* Mary promised at Fatima.

This Crusade should be a unified effort among all the different movements in the Church, not just those that are Marian or dedicated to the Rosary. I also pray this Crusade will be officially *"blessed"* by the Holy Father.

Through prayer, I believe God is calling for this mighty effort. Please find below the addresses and phone numbers of several different Rosary organizations that are now organizing Rosary Crusades.

> National Rosary Crusade
> The Blue Army, U.S.A.
> P.O. Box 976
> Washington, NJ. 07882
> (For Material, call (908) 689-1700
>
> ———————————
>
> The Perpetual Rosary Crusade
> Robert H. Kessler
> P.O. Box 345
> Dayton, OH. 45419

SELECTED BIBLIOGRAPHY

——. *A Man Called Jozo*. Milford, Ohio: The Riehle Foundation, 1989.

Brown, Michael H. *The Final Hour*. Milford, Ohio: Faith Publishing Company, 1992.

Bettwy, Sr. Isabel. *I am the Guardian of the Faith*. Steubenville, Ohio; Franciscan University Press, 1991.

Casalletto, Thomas, *A State of Emergency*, Richardson and Steirman, New York, 1987

Connell, Jan. *Queen of the Cosmos*. Orlean, Massachusetts: Paraclete Press, 1990.

De Monfort, Saint Louis. *Secret of the Rosary*. Bay Shore, New York: Montfort Publications, 1984

De Monfort, Saint Louis. *True Devotion to Mary*. Rockfor Illinois: Tan Books and Publishers, 1985

Flynn, Ted and Maureen. *The Thunder of Justice*. Sterling, Virginia: MaxKol Communications, Inc., 1993.

Gobbi, Don Stefano. *Our Lady Speaks to Her Beloved Priests*. St. Francis, Maine: The Nations Headquarters of the Marian Movement of Priests in the United States of America, 1988.

Gribble, Richard C.C., *The History and Devotion of the Rosary*, Our Sunday Visitor, Hunington, Indiana, 1992.

Haffert, John M. *Her Own Words to the Nuclear Age*. Asbury, New Jersey: Lay Apostalate Foundation, 1993.

Haffert, John M. *The Meaning of Akita*. Asbury, New Jersey: 101 Foundation, Inc., 1989.

Haffert, John M. *To Prevent This*. Asbury, New Jersey: 101 Foundation, Inc., 1993.

John Paul II, Pope. *Crossing the Threshold of Hope*. New York: Alfred a. Knopf, 1994.

Kelly, Matthew. *Words from God*. Batesman Bay, N.S.W., Australia, 1993

—— Kolbe, St. Maximilian, *Aim Higher*, Prow Books/Fransican Marytown Press. Libertyville, Illinois, 1994.

Laurentin, Rene. *The Apparitions of the Blessed Virgin Mary Today*, Paris France, Veritas Publications 1991.

Martin, Jacov. *Queen of Peace in Medjugorje*. Milford, Ohio: The Riehle Foundation, 1989.

Martin, Malachi. *The Keys of This Blood*. New York: Touchstone - Simon and Schuster, 1990.

Natalia, Sr. Maria. *The Victorious Queen of the World*. (The spiritual diary of a contemporary mystic, Sr Natalia of Hungary) Mountain View, California: Queen Publishing, 1993.

Nolan, Denis, Medjugorje, *A Time for Truth, A Time for Action*, Santa Barbara, California, Queenship Publishing, 1993.

Petrisko, Thomas W. *Call of the Ages*. Santa Barbara, California: Queenship Publishing Company, 1995.

Petrisko, Thomas W. *For the Soul of the Family*. (unpublished as of present date)

Petrisko, Thomas W. (editor) *Our Lady Queen of Peace* - Special Edition I. Pittsburgh, Pennsylvania: Pittsburgh Center for Peace, Inc., 1991

Petrisko, Thomas W. (editor) *Our Lady Queen of Peace* - Special Edition II. Pittsburgh, Pennsylvania: Pittsburgh Center for Peace, Inc., 1992.

Petrisko, Thomas W. (editor) *Our Lady Queen of Peace* - Special Edition III. Pittsburgh, Pennsylvania: Pittsburgh Center for Peace, Inc., 1995.

Petrisko, Thomas W. *The Sorrow, the Sacrifice, and the Triumph, The Apparitions, Visions and Prophecies of Christina Gallagher*. New York: Simon and Schuster, Inc., 1995.

Shamon, Rev Albert J.M, *The Power of the Rosary*, Milford, Ohio, The Riehle Foundation, 1990.

Terelya, Josyp with Michael H. Brown. *Witness*. Milford, Ohio: Faith Publishing Company, 1991.

——. *The Holy Bible Douay Rheims Version*. Rockford, Illinois: TAN Books and Publishing, Inc.

—— *The New American Bible*, Witchita, Kansas: Catholic Bible Publishers, 1984-1985 Edition

NOTES

CHAPTER 7: A Breaking Dawn

The messages to Father Gobbi in this chapter and throughout the book came from *Our Lady Speaks to Her Beloved Priests* and are used with permission. The messages to Christina Gallagher come from the books, *Please Come Back to Me and My Son* by R. Vincent and *The Sorrow, The Sacrifice and the Triumph* by the author. Josyp Terelya's messages come from the book *Witness* by Josyp Terelya and Michael Brown. The messages to Sister Natalie comes from the book *Victorious Queen of the World*. The messages to Estela Ruiz are from the book *Our Lady of the Americas*. The messages to Patricia Talbot are from *I am the Guardian of the Faith* by Sister Isabelle Bettwy. The message to Sister Agnes Sassagawa is from *Akita the Tears and Messages*. The message from Jesus to Madeleine is from *Dozule's the Unique and Definitive Messages of Christ*.

EPILOGUE

The messages from Medjugorje are from the Newspaper, Our Lady Queen of Peace, *Special Editions I,II,III* published by the Pittsburgh Center for Peace. St. Louis De Montfort's quotes are from the books *True Devotion, The Secret of the Rosary* and *Our Lady Queen of Peace Special Edition II*.

ABOUT THE COVER

After a pilgrimage to Medjugorje, cover artist and designer, Gerry Simboli, found that most of the assignments coming her way were of a spiritual nature. She has designed and illustrated video jackets for "Marian Apparitions of the 20th Century", "The Fathers's Gift" and a new video about the effects of abortion called "Don't Cry Mary", "The Bridge to Heaven" book jacket is also her work. Gerry and husband, Joe, a talented designer and woodworker, have created sculpted religious works in wood. One of their creations is the Mother of the Holy Eucharist monstrance where the Mother of God, with humility and in shadow, holds the luna containing the blessed sacrament over her heart.

For further information about this monstrance, you may write to:
Simboli Design
Box 26
Cheyney, PA 19319
(610) 399-0156

Best Sellers by Dr. Thomas W. Petrisko!

THE FATIMA PROPHECIES
At the Doorstep of the World

Beginning approximately ten years before the French Revolution, Dr. Thomas Petrisko takes a look at the hundreds of apparitions and miracles that occurred in the nineteenth century all the way up to the apparitions at Fatima in 1917. Confronted is the rise of Communism and nuclear warfare in association with the two unfulfilled prophecies of Fatima: the annihilation of nations and the Era of Peace. Written in a fast moving, popular style, this book also tells of the many contemporary prophecies and apparitions and how they point toward the fulfillment of Fatima. *ISBN: 1-891903-06-3, 486 pp.*

Only $12.95

THE MIRACLE OF THE ILLUMINATION OF ALL CONSCIENCES

From as far back as the 16th century, when St. Edmund Campion of England spoke of *"a great day that would reveal all men's consciences,"* a coming "day of enlightenment" has been foretold. It is purported to be a day in which God will supernaturally illuminate the conscience of every man, woman, and child on earth. Each person, then, would momentarily see the state of their soul through God's eyes and realize the truth of His existence. This predicted event is now said to be imminent, as talk concerning the certainty of this miracle has intensified. *ISBN: 1-891903-25-X, 164 pp.*

Only $10.95

Toll-Free (888) 654-6279 or (412) 787-9735 www.SaintAndrew.com

Best Sellers by Dr. Thomas W. Petrisko!

INSIDE HEAVEN AND HELL
What History, Theology, and the Mystics tell us about the Afterlife

Beginning with death and judgment, bestselling author Dr. Thomas Petrisko takes us on a spiritual journey with the saints, mystics, visionaries, and the Blessed Mother - inside Heaven and Hell. Will you be ready come Judgment Day? Discover what really happens at your judgment and how everything you say and do will be a cause for your eternal reward or, perhaps, your everlasting punishment. With profound new insight into what awaits each one of us, this book is a **must read for all those who are serious about earning their 'salvation.'**

Only $12.95

ISBN: 1-891903-23-3, 204 pp.

INSIDE PURGATORY
What History, Theology, and the Mystics tell us about Purgatory

Today there is little mention of Purgatory, even among Catholics. It is, however, a teaching handed down from the Apostles and found in Sacred Scripture. Purgatory is said to be a necessary part of the justice of God, which responds to all sin. The Church teaches that even the least sin displeases God. Thus, His mercy, which pardons, contains His justice, which cleanses. Purgatory, therefore, is a place of justice. May all who read this book come to know the truth about Purgatory, how each of us face the possibility of going there if not purified of the stain of our sins before death, and how the countless souls there are waiting for our help to get them into Heaven. ISBN: 1-891903-24-1, 128 pp.

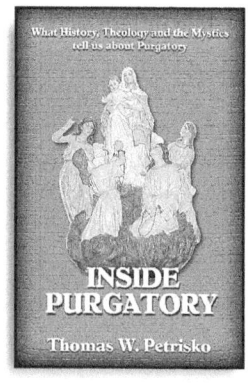

Only $8.95

Toll-Free (888) 654-6279 or (412) 787-9735 www.SaintAndrew.com

Made in United States
North Haven, CT
21 June 2023

38070568R00049